Fund-raising is like dieting—it's easier said than done! Successful fund-raising requires a well thought out plan, a step-by-step approach, and a true understanding of why people donate money. In my 35 years of fundraising, I have never found a book that covers all that territory. Until now! William Bradshaw has written a book that should be on every fund-raiser's desk, from novice to veteran. He fully understands that successful fund-raising is a process that anyone can learn. If you want to guarantee a bigger dollar return for your hard work, this is the book.

Charles B. Inlander
President, People's Medical Society
Faculty lecturer, Yale University School of Medicine

As Chairman of the Board of Trustees of Lees Co[illegible] and Chairman and President of the bank the college did bu[illegible] it was my pleasure to observe the outstanding fund-r[illegible] of Dr. Bradshaw. I was always amazed when he could g[illegible] people and organizations that never gave before. Without a doubt, he is the best fund-raiser with whom I have ever worked or known.

J. Phil Smith, Chairman and President
First National Bank, Jackson, KY

After years of observing William Bradshaw's successful fund-raising efforts on behalf of many different entities, I applaud this publication sharing the steps he follows to bring about success in meeting the needs of non-profit organizations. This book will guide the novice as well as the experienced fund-raiser as they compete for funding sources. It has particular relevance for college and university courses devoted to fund-raising and the development of those who will keep alive the concept of giving on behalf of worthwhile causes for the common good.

Velma B. Saire, Ed. D., Adjunct Professor
H. John Heinz III School of Public Policy and Management
Carnegie Mellon University

In selecting the person to spearhead the fund-raising efforts of our foundation in the United States, we looked for someone who can make things happen, who has documented experience as an effective fundraiser, and who has the ability to lead and motivate others. Dr. Bradshaw is that person. He gets the job done!

F. W. de Klerk
Chairperson, the FW de Klerk Foundation
Former President of the Republic of South Africa

One realizes immediately that Dr. Bradshaw has been an effective and efficient fundraiser, and I applaud him for taking the time to put his 12 step process in the written form for others to learn from. The book offers something for every fundraiser, from the novice to expert. As someone who has been fundraising for close to fifteen years, reading this book served as a refresher course and a thought provoking experience. It is a wonderful new resource for the incredible field of development.

Ruth L. Lederman, Director of Development
Jewish Federation of St. Louis, MO

In my roles as a graduate student, college-board member, and pastor I have had varying degrees of responsibility for raising over $82 million. However, Dr. Bradshaw's book is the first formal instruction I have ever had in this important work of fund-raising. This practical, readable (I love the stories!), and encouraging book is long overdue in my life. I can now be enthusiastic about raising funds for projects about which I am passionate! This fellow pastor has taught me that advancing institutions boils down to this: trust God, dignify people, and work with professionalism.

The Reverend Mr. George W. Robertson
Senior Pastor, The Covenant Presbyterian Church of St. Louis
Adjunct Professor of Homiletics, Covenant Theological Seminary

---

Fund-raising is neither art nor science; it is instead relationship, relationship, relationship. William Bradshaw knows this well and in this book has carefully shared a system of fund-raising that has emerged from a wealth of personal experience. This book is a helpful reminder for all who raise funds about the need to attend to the essentials. For those just beginning work in fundraising, this book is a great place from which to launch. The author is passionate about fund-raising for many reasons but mostly, because he says, “The more money we raise, the more lives we can affect.”

Dr. David Greenhaw, President
Eden Theological Seminary
St. Louis, MO

Here is one of the most comprehensive books I have seen on fund-raising. It covers all the bases in a most sensitive and caring manner. Building good relationships along the way is the book's real bonus. To help people feel good about giving to worthy causes is a real gift. Dr. Bradshaw has made this a top priority. This well could be a classic in the art of fund-raising.

The Reverend Dr. William O Smith
Phoenix, AZ

FUNDRAISING

the SYSTEM *that* WORKS

William B. Bradshaw, Ph.D.

Pittsburgh, PA

ISBN 1-58501-084-7

Trade Paperback

Second Printing—2004
Library of Congress #2004105679

Request for information should be addressed to:

SterlingHouse Publisher, Inc.
7436 Washington Avenue
Pittsburgh, PA 15218
www.sterlinghousepublisher.com

CeShore is an imprint of SterlingHouse Publisher, Inc.

SterlingHouse Publisher, Inc. is a company
of the CyntoMedia Corporation

Art Director: Matthew J. Lorenz
Cover Design: Matthew J. Lorenz - SterlingHouse Publisher
Typesetting & Layout Design: N. J. McBeth
Illustration/Cover Art: Matthew J. Lorenz

Printed in the United States of America

ACKNOWLEDGEMENTS

I have often wondered why nearly all recipients of Academy Awards feel compelled to thank so many people. Now I understand. There are many individuals I would like to thank for their help and encouragement when I was writing this book. I will, however, limit my comments to three people.

Our daughter Rebekah gave unselfishly of her time to read every sentence of the book with the critical eye of an editor. She re-wrote awkward sentences and shortened overly-long stories. She rearranged the format of the book and made it much easier to read and understand.

Velma Saire, Ed. D., an outstanding educator and former colleague, helped in researching material, verifying facts, making final editorial suggestions, and identifying publishing companies that possibly would be interested in this book.

My wife, Betty June, was at my side throughout my career, and she helped refresh my memory about the details of many of the incidents mentioned in the book. She was the first person to read each chapter of the book, making helpful suggestions and correcting misspellings. Although I will get the credit for developing the fund-raising system that serves as the core of this book, Betty June was very much involved in my career and deserves to share in the credit.

I would have had trouble writing this book without their help, and I question whether any publisher would have accepted it for publication had all three of these people not been involved. I find it difficult to express adequately my heartfelt appreciation and gratitude. To the three of you, I say a very special "Thank you."

William B. Bradshaw

TABLE OF CONTENTS

CHAPTER 3

Step 3: Think of yourself as a matchmaker **31**

CHAPTER 4

Step 4: Concentrate on the number of gifts instead of the dollar amounts of gifts **45**

CHAPTER 5

CHAPTER 6

CHAPTER 7

CHAPTER 8

CHAPTER 9

CHAPTER 10

INTRODUCTION

I have been a very successful fund-raiser over the course of my career working for and with charitable institutions and not-for-profit (NFP) organizations. My success as a fundraiser began with a rather insignificant conversation during a significant time in my life. My father was a patient battling cancer at the Mayo Clinic in Rochester, Minnesota. I had the opportunity to meet with a senior administrator at the Clinic. I asked him, "What makes Mayo Clinic so successful?"

He was quick to answer. "It is not, as many people think, that we pay the highest salaries to our doctors. Doctors in private practice can make more money than they do at the Mayo Clinic. Nor is it because we have the best facilities and equipment in the world, although ours are very adequate. Instead, it is because of the *system* we use. In fact, any group of doctors, any place in our country or the world, could have a Mayo Clinic if they used our system. Importantly, we never compromise the system either in diagnosing or in treating disease." He then explained that the Mayo brothers developed the basic elements of the system, which have been refined through the years.

At the time, I was relatively young and in the early stages of my career. I was a parish minister and board member of other small not-for-profit (NFP) organizations. I was well aware of the consistent difficulty most charitable organizations and institutions had in acquiring adequate funds for operating purposes. My conversation with the administrator at the Mayo Clinic caused me to wonder if a system existed for funding NFPs: a system that would accurately diagnose reasons for financial shortfalls, a system that would determine how to overcome shortfalls and provide adequate funding, and a system that would work equally well for NFPs regardless of their nature or purpose.

After extensive research, I did not find such a system. Believing that such a system would be of immeasurable help to NFPs, I decided to develop one. Much to my surprise it was considerably more difficult than I anticipated. Initially, I assumed I could think through what seemed to be the logical steps of successful fund-raising. I discovered, however, that what we sometimes think will happen in fund-raising frequently does not (not a big surprise to most of you in the fund-raising world). Although many of the principles remain the same, the system for fund-raising that I use today has been greatly revised from my initial version.

The System, as I have come to call it, is based on my 35+ years of experiences as a college president, the development officer for a community college, the minister of large city churches, and as an independent consultant for numerous agencies and institutions. ***The System*** is the result of years of real-life fund-raising experiences used to identify, test, refine, and articulate the necessary steps for consistently being a successful fund-raiser. It is a culmination of the many successes and pitfalls I encountered along the way. It is a system that has worked for me, has worked for institutions with whom I have consulted, and it can work for you.

The System will work across the gamut of NFPs: churches, synagogues, YMCAs, nursing homes, colleges/schools, libraries, museums, special purpose clubs, international organizations, social service agencies, youth groups, campgrounds, national charities, performing arts, environmental groups, relief organizations, AIDS prevention, and on the list goes. ***The system*** works regardless of the purpose for which the money is being sought: operating budget, annual fund, capital campaign, special purpose drive, planned giving, equipping computer labs, contingencies, etc. ***The system*** works!

I do not mean to suggest that by waving a magic wand all your financial woes will disappear and that you and your organization will automatically raise unlimited funds.

The System is a sound step-by-step process that serves as a foundation for successful fund-raising. With ***The System*** you will be able to do the following things:

- Realistically recognize and evaluate your financial needs;
- Plan realistic short- and long-term funding strategies;
- Select and employ committed staff;

- Identify funding sources that are likely to contribute to your particular cause;
- Learn how to select, use, and tailor the most effective methods of asking donors in order to assure the best results with each individual prospect;
- Promptly implement specific programs that will generate immediate dollars;
- Attract the funds needed to meet long-term needs; and
- Best of all, create good will among your contributors, thus establishing a strong base of repeat givers.

Most of us know that fund-raising has many inherent pressures. It is a daunting responsibility to be the person with whom "the buck stops" when raising the funds that are absolutely essential for a charitable agency, organization, or institution to continue operating and fulfilling its mission. By using ***The System*** consistently and in its entirety you can be relatively certain that you will achieve your immediate fund-raising goals and enhance the prospects for long-range financial stability. Your margin of success will be in direct proportion to the degree you remain true to the basic elements of ***The System***. The more you compromise or "short-cut" ***The System*** the less money you are likely to raise. Likewise, the truer you remain to ***The System*** the more money you are likely to raise.

Three incidents—unfortunately all negative—caused me to write this book. Negative incident #1 occurred about five years ago when I went to visit the new development officer of a local religious-affiliated liberal arts college. I wanted to welcome him to the city and offer to help him, if he ever wanted or needed an experienced and impartial sounding board. When I entered his office he was obviously busy, and it soon became apparent to me that he was more interested in getting back to his computer than in talking with me. In short, he "thanked" me for my offer but declined by saying to me, "The greatest contribution you old guys can make to today's fund-raising efforts is to write a book." Needless to say, I took his comment more as a "put-down" than as a legitimate request for input from a seasoned fund-raising professional.

Although I resented the "old-guy" comment from this development officer (who I would like to think was overwhelmed and overworked), it did plant the seed to write a book. And as I observed the financial demise of this institution over the next several years, I became increasingly sensitive to the need for such a book. Early in my career I struggled to raise money and to increase outreach to people. I would have loved to have had the input and guidance from other fund-raisers with proven track records. It took two more incidents, however, to convince me of the absolute need for this book.

The second reason for writing the book is that charitable giving is suffering as a result of September 11, 2001, and those responsible for giving and receiving charitable funds need as much help and encouragement as possible. After that horrible terrorist attack, there was a literal outpouring of financial resources from people all over our country. Some people gave directly to entities they were personally acquainted with, while others gave to existing relief organizations or foundations, relying on them to distribute the money to those in need. The United States Government, families, and NFPs established new funds to help people who had been directly or indirectly affected by 9/11. Several things resulted from this outpouring of concern and generosity.[1] The most obvious was that individuals gave so generously to the 9/11 efforts that their contributions to other charitable causes were curtailed. Initially, foundations and corporations continued their charitable giving at pre-9/11 levels, but gradually a majority of foundations and many corporations also curtailed their giving.[2]

Many NFPs, large and small, have experienced a decline in the number and dollar value of charitable gifts received.[3] To add to this hurdle, legitimate questions began to surface concerning how some relief agencies or organizations were distributing their funds. Many donors felt that some 9/11 relief organizations were not using the monies received for the purposes for which they were given. It also became obvious that many well-intending people just were not equipped or qualified to handle the magnitude and complexity of the tasks at hand. And questions arose about the procedures the United States Government was using in determining who should receive relief funds and how much they should receive. These factors led to the increased scrutiny of the entire NFP sector. Unfortunately (and in most instances unfairly) disillusionment, doubt, and a lack of trust about charitable giving in general began to creep into the picture. As a result, many very worthwhile organizations and institutions are facing a severe financial shortfall and are likely to face this problem for some time to come. They need help now.

The third reason for writing this book is our economic downturn and the overall decline in the value of stocks and other investments. As stock portfolios declined, many institutions have seen their endowment funds decline proportionately in value, resulting in less income now and in the foreseeable future.[4] Likewise, individuals and foundations have seen their portfolios decline in value, and they do not have the funds currently available to sustain their previous levels of charitable giving. Further, corporations have had to pull back from their previous levels of charitable giving. NFPs are experiencing substantially fewer gifts and of lesser value than in the past. It is unnerving because nobody knows how long it will take for the economy to recover and for stock prices to rebound. And, when they do rebound, much lasting damage will have been done; eroding effects of these factors on fund-raising will linger long after the economy has fully recovered.

Today, NFPs are needed more than ever, and most of them are struggling financially more than ever. I am firmly convinced that ***The System*** can guide and assist in raising the millions and millions of dollars needed by the NFPs—thus helping people and making this a better world in which to live.

This book will help both the fund-raiser and the fund-giver obtain their goals. ***The System*** will provide a strong foundation that can be depended upon in building and sustaining successful charitable giving efforts. Especially since 9/11, there should be no doubt about it—the vast majority of American people are by nature generous, and they want to contribute their financial resources when there is a need and when they can possibly afford to do so. As Americans are increasingly becoming more dependent on and supportive of NFPs, ***The System*** is becoming a more valuable tool for fund-raisers to use in their quest for charitable gifts and for potential contributors to use in their desire to contribute to the causes close to their hearts.

The captain and first officer of commercial airplanes have an entire network of checklists they rely on to keep airplanes as safe as possible.[5] They have checklists for every aspect of flying: to assure all systems are in order prior to starting the engines, to start the engines, to taxi the runway, to take off, to fly, to land. Most of the checklists are referred to as "challenge-and-response" checklists—that is, one person reads the item to be checked and the other responds. One could make a reasonably strong case for suggesting that these checklists are not needed. After all, pilots go through these procedures every time they fly, and they do not need a checklist to know what to do. But nearly every captain and first officer will be the first to tell you how important these checklists are. They are important not because the cockpit crew learns anything new from them, but just to make absolutely certain that the crew, on all of their flights, takes every single step that is required to take off and land safely—that none is accidentally omitted.

The System can be compared to the checklists used in flying airplanes. ***The System*** involves 12 specific steps that need to be completed and checked off one by one for every fund-raising endeavor. If we take the results of our fund-raising and fund-giving as seriously as we want pilots to take their flying, we will welcome the discipline dictated by ***The System***—just to make absolutely certain that every step needed for successful fund-raising is taken, that none is accidentally omitted. This holds true even for the seasoned fund-raising professional for whom little of this may be new.

All pilots also have a *Jeppesen Manual*, a book containing approach charts for every airport used. These manuals are updated weekly. The checklists referred to above remain constant for each airplane; the various Jeppesen charts, on the other hand, change from airport to airport, as each airport is different and must be approached accordingly. Similarly, the players and scenarios in fund-raising differ from one project to the next and must be managed accordingly, but the basics remain the same.

The System is this never-changing network of steps that can be depended upon for success in all fund-raising endeavors. Although it is impossible to foresee and discuss the details of every potential fund-raising event, ***The System*** will provide everyone—from the well-seasoned fund-raiser to the beginner—with the unchanging foundation to work out and apply the appropriate details of every funding effort. Whether one is participating in the annual fund drive, a special campaign for operating expenses, a capital campaign for new buildings, an effort to build the endowment fund, or whatever, ***The System***, if followed, will definitely make a positive difference. More money will be raised, and the contributors will be happier.

This book is not a manual to keep you up to date on tax laws and other regulations relating to charitable giving. It is expected that you will turn to regulatory publications, seminars, training literature, CD ROMs, on-line sources, lawyers, accountants, and financial advisors to keep you abreast of all such pertinent information. This book and ***The System*** address a specific process or way of approaching one's fund-raising efforts, assuming that you will always take into consideration current laws. Unless there are very drastic changes in the charitable giving laws of our country, the periodic changing of such laws will not affect the use and effectiveness of ***The System***. During the 35 years that I have been using ***The System***, there have been many far-reaching changes in the tax laws, usually to the disadvantage of charitable giving. Yet none of these changes has altered the development and use of ***The System***, except to make it more valuable.

In addition to the Introduction, the book is divided into 12 chapters, each devoted to one step of ***The System***, and the Conclusion that ties the details together. Although there are 12 different steps to ***The System***, and we will examine each step in detail, the success of ***The System*** depends upon thinking of all of the steps working together as a coordinated effort. The book is relatively short and easy to read, and your results will definitely be enhanced if you read all 12 chapters before trying to put into practice any single step of ***The System***.

As you read this book and concentrate on each of the 12 individual steps of ***The System***, you must keep in focus the following five fundamentals of sound fund-raising. These five basic principles are essential to the success of all fund-raising endeavors and are part of the infrastructure for the entirety of ***The System***.

1. **Focus a majority of your time on people.** Successful fund-raisers will spend a majority of their time and effort focused on people, with less time spent appealing to foundations and corporations. Historically, approximately 85% of all charitable contributions from private (nongovernmental) sources come from individuals.[6] Far too frequently fund-raisers make the mistake of focusing their primary efforts on foundations and corporations, which on average account for only 15% of all charitable contributions, far less than the contributions from individuals.

2. **Successful fund-raisers are good listeners.** Remember, God created us with two ears and only one mouth. Many fund-raisers are guilty of spending too much time talking and "pitching" the merits of their own cause, organization, or institution. Instead, they need to listen intently to what the prospective contributors are saying. That is how you learn about their values, their goals in life, and their thoughts. And that is how you raise money.

3. **Serve the best interest of your contributors.** In the end, the most important goal in fund-raising is not how much money is raised, but whether the best interests of the contributors are served. It is difficult to keep this one in focus, especially if your institution is hard put for money or your job is on the line. If you are going to be successful year after year and have the respect of your peers and the general public, you must always do what is best for the contributors.

4. **Teamwork is essential to successful fund-raising.** It takes the combined efforts of many people working together to raise needed funds consistently over the long haul. Teamwork is needed on

three different levels: between the fund-raiser and the fund-giver, within the NFP, and among NFPs.

The fund-raiser and the fund-giver must always be on the same page. It is important for family members of the fund-giver to be involved so that they do not get caught by surprise and try to circumvent what is being planned. Frequently the team will also need to include the fund-giver's attorney, accountant, or financial advisor. If you are afraid to involve them, you most likely know that you are treading on thin ice.

Within bigger organizations or institutions the team will include several members of the fund-raising staff, as well as the participation of other departments, the administration, and volunteers. Successful fund-raisers must receive their satisfaction not from being the center of attraction as the one always asking for contributions, but from quietly orchestrating the entire process and being certain to involve the other people needed to get the job done and who will, therefore, share the pride and the limelight.

And it is important for all charitable organizations to remember that although they are in competition with each other for receiving charitable contributions, the entire NFP sector needs to work together as a team for the good of all legitimate charitable causes.

5. **Every organization or institution raising money must be concerned about both current and future financial security.** To insure the integrity of the NFP and long-term support from contributors, successful fund-raisers must be certain that how and for what the monies are raised and utilized will make a positive and lasting impression on all people involved. That makes it so much more feasible to raise the needed funds the next time around.

Without question, keeping these five fundamentals in mind will increase your success as a fund-raiser or fund-giver. ***The System*** will guide you through the process.

Through the years I have heard fund-raisers routinely encourage their donors to "Give until it hurts." This statement has always bothered me. Whenever I hear it I ask myself, "Whom do you want to hurt—the donor, the donee, the people the charitable entity helps, or all of them?" I like, instead, to think that charitable giving helps. And that is exactly what the end result of using ***The System*** will be. Everyone involved will be helped.

The System does not deal with fund-raising for just any organization. ***The System*** focuses specifically on securing funds for **charitable** organizations, institutions, agencies, and causes. Fund-raising professionals in the NFP sector look beyond the raising of money to what the funds will be used for. They focus on the ultimate goal of making this world a better place in which to live. Using ***The System*** can help you become a legitimate member of the team of people who devotes their lives to making that goal a reality.

NOTES TO THE INTRODUCTION

1. Reports and statistics relating to the aftermath of 9/11 suggest different findings and conclusions. It will take a few years to evaluate accurately both the direct and indirect ramifications of 9/11 on charitable giving. Based on materials currently available, there is no question in this writer's mind that 9/11 has had an immediate adverse effect on charitable giving that will continue to be felt for many years. For various opinions about the effect of 9/11 on charitable giving see: *Giving USA 2002,* a publication of the AAFRC Trust for Philanthropy, researched and written by the Center on Philanthropy at Indiana University, pp, 8-9, 14-15, 19, 20-21, 46-56, 176; *Giving USA 2003,* pp. 54-61; *Giving USA 2004,* pp. 56; *Giving in the Aftermath of 9/11,* a publication by The Foundation Center, Nov., 2002; and *A Survey of Charitable Giving after September 11, 2001,* printed and distributed by Independent Sector, Oct., 2001.

2. Many people suggest that the real causes for lower levels of charitable giving can be traced more to the collapse of the "tech boom," corporate fraud, and a sagging economy than to 9/11 (see note 1). That is partially true. But the aftermath of 9/11 has unquestionably contributed to our economic woes and has adversely impacted our economic recovery, factors that have resulted in less money being available for charitable giving. This conclusion is certainly supported by The Private Bank at Bank of America in a report it published in January, 2003, enti-

tled *Helping You Prosper*. Many industries, especially those related to travel, will never be the same. Also see *Giving USA 2003,* pp. 18-22, 58-60. The fear of future attacks upon our country by terrorists and the active pursuit by the United States Government of terrorist organizations and governments that harbor terrorists have, without question, depressed the stock market and eroded the economic recovery. The war in Iraq has created great uncertainty about the future and has definitely impacted the economic recovery. Many individuals and businesses (both large and small) just do not have the discretionary dollars available for charitable causes. And there are no reputable analysts who suggest that conditions will materially improve anytime in the near future. It seems to me that no one can convincingly argue that the events of 9/11 and their aftermath have not been major culprits in causing (directly and indirectly) fewer charitable dollars being contributed.

3. Historically, initial reports about charitable giving **based on estimates** are issued at the end of each calendar year. It can take up to two years to finalize those reports based on verifiable figures. As the figures for 2002 are being finalized, it appears that data are revealing that charitable giving, adjusted for inflation, declined again in 2002. See *Giving USA 2003,* pp. 6, 8-10, 12-13, 18-26, 62-105; "Giving in 2002 Didn't Outpace Inflation, Report Says," by Harvy Lipman, *The Chronicle of Philanthropy*, pp. 7, 11, 18; "Giving to Education Dropped 1.1% in 2002, Study Finds," by John Pulley, *The Chronicle of Higher Education*, on-line report, June 23, 2003, and "Gifts to Charity in 2002 Stayed Unexpectedly High," by Stephanie Strom, *New York Times*, June 23, 2003, p. A14. In my opinion the title of the story in the *New York Times* is somewhat misleading. The increase in corporate contributions appears to be more because corporations have done a better job of reporting non-monetary gifts—such as services, materials, and products—than actually having contributed more money. I address this subject briefly on page 112.

4. See *The Chronicle of Higher Education:* "College Endowments Had a Negative Return for Second Straight Year, Survey Finds," Dec. 12, 2002; "Another Downer of a Year for College Endowments," Jan. 24, 2003; and "Struggling Against the Tide," Feb. 28, 2003; and *Pittsburgh Post Gazette*, "Endowments Take Collegiate Tumble," Jan. 22, 2003; to mention only four of many such news accounts. Endowments of NFPs in sectors other than education are suffering in the same way.

   However, near the end of 2003 and early in 2004, it appeared that the stock market was on the rebound and that giving to not-for-profits would be upward bound again. See, for example, *Giving USA 2004,* pp. 1-2, 6-47. Since most endowment funds have substantial investments in stocks and bonds, the value of most endowment funds also showed substantial increases. But by mid 2004 that picture had changed considerably. It is also important to keep in mind that receiving one or two very large charitable gifts in a particular year or the loss of one or two major sources of funding in a given year can complicate and confuse the evaluation of trends. It could take several years before we can see a definite and lasting trend relating to the increase or decrease of charitable giving. Regardless of the final outcome, there is no doubt that the events of recent years have had a negative impact on charitable giving.

5. The information about flight procedures in this and following paragraphs was furnished by Mark J. Reinert, pilot for Ozark Airlines and TWA.

6. This includes outright gifts and bequests. The statistics show that these figures have varied from year to year, and historically the total from individuals has ranged from 75 to 85%. *Giving USA* reports that giving by individuals (including bequests) accounted for 82.96% of all charitable giving in 2001, 83% in 2002, and 83.5% in 2003. Foundation grants accounted for 11.9% of all charitable contributions in 2001, 11.5% in 2002, and 10.9% in 2003. Corporate gifts came in at 5.1% in 2001, 5.5% in 2002, and 5.6% in 2003. See *Giving USA 2002, 2003,* and *2004* for details, especially pp. 48-55 of *Giving USA 2004.* One can find estimates for giving by individuals from other sources, but there is no question that *Giving USA* is the source most frequently quoted.

   The Foundation Center is the most authoritative source for information about foundation grants and corporate charitable giving. LexisNexis, a division of Reed Elsevier Inc., does a very creditable job of collecting reliable data from various sources, including *Giving USA* and The Foundation Center, and displaying the statistics in tables and charts that are easy to understand and that can be accessed online at lexis-nexis.com. *Giving to Yale: 2001-2002,* p. 29, published by Yale University at the close of 2002, indicates that giving from individuals was at about 80% and from foundations and corporations at 20%.

   The current trend seems to indicate increased giving by individuals and corporations, and decreased giving by foundations. But as pointed out in note 4, one should be careful about declaring trends too quickly.

CHAPTER 1

STEP 1: PLAN YOUR WORK, AND WORK YOUR PLAN.

One day in a small but vital Midwestern city, a member of the large Baptist Church called the church office and asked to speak with the minister. The church secretary told the parishioner that the minister was busy reading a book. Unless it was an emergency, he was unable to take the phone call, but he would call back later that day. Thinking that the minister was putting his own frivolous needs above those of the congregation, the parishioner became irate and within days called for the resignation of the minister. Needless to say, this caused considerable disruption in the congregation and served as a frequent topic of conversation throughout the community.

Unfortunately, this represents the limited views of many people: if you are reading and thinking during office hours, you are being unproductive. Had the secretary told this person that the minister was in a meeting, teaching a class, in a counseling session, or doing any number of things other than reading a book, there would have been no problems. Reading books should be done on his own time—during off hours.

Church membership had grown significantly under this minister's leadership, to no small degree because his sermons were provocative, challenging, and filled with information from a wide variety of sources. Although some of his fellow ministers differed with him on some theological issues, they agreed he was a very effective preacher, as did members and non-members of his church. Ironically, what set this minister apart from his fellow ministers was his disciplined approach to scheduling time each week to read and study, without which it would have been impossible for him to have had cutting-edge sermons every Sunday.

Do not Leave it to Chance—Schedule Your Planning Time

Thorough planning is absolutely essential for effective fund-raising. Unfortunately, NFPs frequently find themselves in a catch-22: they cannot raise money until they have a well-thought-out fund-raising plan, but without adequate money they cannot take the time or employ the personnel needed to help devise successful fund-raising plans. But any person who is to be successful at fund-raising must find a way to participate in the planning phase of raising money.

A very common complaint among executives is not having adequate time to think, plan, and develop strategies. They do not have time to be proactive and plan for the future because they are too busy taking care of immediate needs and problems. Regular staff meetings are effective for making short-range plans, sharing information, and providing updates, but they do not allow the time or provide the setting needed for in-depth discussions and long-range planning.

To have uninterrupted, focused planning time, organizations and institutions have long relied on off-site meetings or retreats. In previous decades it was common practice for executives and their staffs to go on planning retreats that lasted several days and were often held at out-of-town locations, perhaps at a rustic camp or resort. But given today's pressures "at the office," the trend is toward shorter off-site meetings. Today, many organizations allow for only a half-day meeting, generally at a nearby hotel so that participants may work a half-day in the office. The need to plan is crucial, but we are programmed to let our day-to-day pressures squeeze out planning time.

Plan Strategically, Holistically, and Politically

The planning process will usually include several different plans, depending upon the volume and diversity of funding activities being pursued. Each NFP needs a comprehensive, strategic plan that outlines its entire development effort. Equally as important, the development strategic plan must be integrated with the overall strategic plan of the organization to ensure a consistency of mission, goals, messages, and activities. Also needed is an individual plan for each development project undertaken by the organization. Finally, each of these plans must be coordinated and integrated with each other. The plan for the annual campaign, for example, must be consistent with the overall strategic plan of the entire development office, with the plans for all other individual funding projects, and with the goals, mission, and activities of the organization as a whole. This is similarly true when an NFP is conducting a campaign for any other purpose.

Careful planning is very time consuming, but it is crucial for good fund-raising. In all likelihood it will slow the process of getting a funding project started and can also cause dissension in the ranks (from above or below). Because of this, fund-raisers are sometimes tempted to take shortcuts in the planning process. However, not taking the time for thorough planning prior to beginning a funding effort is shortsighted.

Determine When to Bring In Outside Professionals

Through the years, my family moved frequently for my job, and we remodeled several houses. Additionally, as the minister of several large churches and as a college president, it was my responsibility to oversee a variety of capital improvements: such things as finding room for a new pipe organ, remodeling and refurbishing entire buildings, demolishing old buildings, building additions to existing structures, rebuilding a campground dining room and dormitories destroyed by fire, and constructing parking facilities. We will not mention the necessary and acquired skills for fixing copying machines, replacing windows, painting, and dealing with bats and rodents. Early on in my career (both through successes and failures), I learned the necessity for thorough planning prior to starting any building or remodeling process.

I also learned the importance of using specialists in various fields, even though this may lead to controversy for two reasons: disagreement over whom to use and the perceived expense of employing outside professionals. Many people, for example, think that the use of architects and professional interior designers by NFPs is too expensive for remodeling projects. However, not using professionals can ultimately be both more expensive and stressful. The fees of these professionals often prove to be far less costly than the money required to rectify the structural and aesthetic problems created by not using them. Furthermore, I can guarantee that designing buildings and selecting colors by committees is certain to lead to hurt feelings and possible loss of good supporters. Strong and sensible leadership usually can overcome the difficulties of selecting the appropriate professionals, but frequently large doses of tact and diplomacy are called for.

Just as good planning is essential for any construction project, it is also essential for fund-raising. The planning process for fund-raising will be time-consuming and possibly expensive, depending on your need for outside professionals or consultants to balance your in-house staff. But having a complete set of fund-raising blueprints in writing before starting a project will help eliminate disappointing and damaging results, including embarrassing surprises, mistakes, hurt feelings, unfavorable publicity, and a financial shortfall. Thorough planning sessions are time consuming, can be tedious, and may prolong the targeted start of a project. But in the long run, you will save time and money, your results will more likely reach expectations, and your contributors will be happier.

An older man who was my development mentor for many years, said it more succinctly: "The plan is what makes the mule plow." In other words, the plan is what makes any fund-raising effort actually happen.

Realistically Plan Your Time, and Be Specific

On college campuses, students commonly request extensions for term papers. They procrastinate or underestimate how long it will take to write a really good paper. They think they will be able to sit down at the computer and get it done in an evening or two. But once students get started, they realize that they have only general concepts and sketchy ideas and lack the specific facts and figures—the real meat of the term paper. Prior to committing their thoughts to final written form, the students need additional time to transform their random ideas into specific concepts supported by critical thinking and verifiable research.

This is what frequently happens in the fund-raising process. We have general ideas of how we are going to raise money, the people we will contact, and the resources we will use, but it is not until we actually write our plans that we turn vague ideas into concrete blueprints from which to work. Far too frequently fund-raisers stumble at the outset of a project or campaign because they have only random ideas about what they are going to do instead of a written document from which to work.

You can bank on this formula: carefully written fund-raising plans equal more effective results. I have seen numerous fund-raisers "wing it" or think through the process as they go along. But I have also seen that fund-raisers attain substantially better results when they devise a plan and commit it to writing before they get started with an endeavor. Having a viable document that serves as a blueprint for those engaged in the fund-raising project assures that the project is better planned, more likely to stay on course, and more apt to yield the desired results.

Whenever you go to a bank to borrow money, the loan officer will ask you two questions, usually in this order: "What are you going to use the money for?" and "How do you plan to pay back the money you borrow?" Unless you have a definite plan on how to use and repay the money, banks will not make the loan. A written plan is essential to secure funding from banks, government agencies, and foundations. Statistics verify that businesses having written plans are much more likely to succeed than those that do not. Likewise, a solid development plan that is committed to writing will help ensure greater results and long-term funding success.

Have a Blueprint Checklist

Successful development officers, like successful builders, have carefully crafted fund-raising blueprints. And they continue to take stock of their fund-raising plans throughout the campaigns or projects, looking at and considering every detail, just as successful builders continue to unroll their blueprints and check for details.

Because NFPs have many different structures and needs, all fund-raising plans are not the same. They apply different methodologies or formats. Just as people approach planning in different ways, so do different NFPs, and what works well for one person or organization may not be the best approach for another. Regardless of the planning format, the following are the key areas of concern that need specifically to be addressed in any fund-raising plan:

1. Purpose for which the money is to be used;
2. Campaign goal, that is, the amount of money needed or desired;
3. Detailed description of how the campaign or event will be organized, executed, concluded, and evaluated;

4. Listing of all personnel needed and their job descriptions (professionals, volunteers, full-time, part-time, committees, clerical, etc.);
5. Complete timetable for all phases of the campaign or event, including such items as planning, appointment of committees, employment of needed personnel, recruitment of volunteers, training, mailing literature and letters, conducting the event, collecting the funds, concluding the campaign, reporting results, and thanking the contributors;
6. Literature and letters that will be needed and who will design them;
7. Budget needed to conduct the event or campaign and where the money will come from;
8. Appropriate giving vehicles to be used by the contributors during this particular campaign;
9. Designation of who will be asking whom;
10. Appropriate records to be kept; and
11. Evaluation procedures.

I cannot stress too strongly the need for development planning to be inclusive, thorough, detailed, and thoughtful in nature. Planning should be done prior to undertaking any major projects. The development planning must be coordinated with all other planning in the organization or institution. And fund-raising plans must result in written documents that can be reviewed, revised, updated, and evaluated.

Be Realistic, and Focus on the Long-Term and Short-Term Needs

It is not enough just to engage in planning. The entire planning process must be grounded in thorough homework and thoughtful deliberation. Impractical plans, regardless of how well intended, are blueprints for failure or, at best, severely diluted results. Occasionally our enthusiasm to succeed and raise money can cloud our judgment, and we end up devising unrealistic programs. This usually happens when we are careless or take shortcuts in doing our homework or "due diligence" prior to undertaking a fund-raising project.

A few years ago, a small private college in a remote and severely economically depressed area employed, as its new president, a dean from a large public university. The new president had never had to raise money and had no experience in doing so. Upon assuming the presidency, he devised a plan to raise most of the four million dollars needed for the college's survival from the local constituency. However, that kind of cash was not available in that rural community of fewer than 3,000 people. The president was right in wanting to involve the local people because it gave them a sense of ownership and inclusion, but it was impractical and unrealistic to expect them to come up with the major share of the money needed.

When fund-raising plans are being devised, one must focus on the organization or institution's immediate needs as well as its long-range financial security. Too frequently, however, NFPs are so under-funded and/or under-staffed that they sacrifice their long-term financial security for immediate financial needs. At the time it may appear that there is no choice other than to designate all contributions for current operating expenditures. In some instances that may be the case. It has been my experience, though, that more frequently it is possible through good fund-raising planning and administrative discipline to meet both immediate and long-term financial needs. But a viable plan needs to be in place that addresses both.

This brings to mind a question that is frequently debated by fundraisers: "If prospective contributors ask (which they often do), should they be encouraged to help underwrite current needs or to invest money for the future by designating their contributions for endowment funds or other long-rang funding endeavors?" Most fund-raisers opt for an undesignated gift. This is my preference. This approach offers the maximum flexibility. The official board of the NFP can use the money however it feels is best, and anytime there is a surplus in its operating budget, the surplus funds can be transferred from the current operating budget to the endowment fund or vice versa.

The problem with this strategy, however, is that people tend to spend most of the money they have on hand rather than save it to assure long-term financial stability (there are always things that would be nice to have now). Unless there is a plan in place that calls for specific amounts of money to be deposited in the endowment fund and other long-term funds, the people controlling the purse strings are more likely to spend money on current operating expenses than they are to put aside adequate funds for long-term financial stability.

It is crucial to have a plan that covers short-term as well as long-term financial needs. Many donors do not care, within reason, what their donations are used for; they just want to make certain that they are used in ways that will be most helpful for the organization or institution. Having a fund-raising plan in place will help that goal to be achieved. The NFP's immediate and long-term needs will already be identified prior to receiving contributions, and spur-of-the-moment decisions on how to use undesignated contributions can be avoided.

Some may make the valid argument that NFPs barely have enough money to meet current expenses, much less to think of trying to save for the future, as worthy as that goal may be. I contend, on the other hand, that if the fund-raising plans have been thorough, complete, and realistic and provide for both current expenses and long-term needs, it is very possible to underwrite current budgets and to set aside money for future needs. In most instances, when those funds are not available it is because no comprehensive, written fund-raising plan was ever adopted and instituted that detailed the specifics of soliciting funds to cover the gamut of needs—current expenses, capital campaigns, endowment funds, and unexpected contingencies. Such a plan will need to designate not only what the contributions are to be used for, but also the sources of the contributions, that is, from individuals (regular contributions and bequests), from foundations, and from corporations.

Two Components of Step 1

Before leaving the subject of planning, I want to emphasize that Step 1 of ***The System*** calls for two specific courses of action. This chapter has, thus far, concentrated on only the first one—planning your work. The second course of action is to work your plan. It is absolutely crucial for every fund-raising effort to have a carefully prepared written plan or blueprint prior to beginning a project, **and** it is essential to work the plan.

I never cease to be amazed at how much money organizations and institutions spend—and then waste—on plans that are never executed. Consultants are frequently engaged at considerable expense, and many, many hours of in-house personnel efforts are invested in crafting elaborate fund-raising plans that are never instituted or get bogged down early on. It happens all the time: a need is identified, a consultant is employed, and a plan is prepared. For one reason or another, no money is raised. The cycle starts again. And every time a new consultant is employed, the first item on the agenda is another feasibility study—an absolute essential, you are told, if the new consultant is to provide you with the counsel and assistance to meet your fund-raising goals. Yes—it is a lot easier to devise a fund-raising plan, or to pay someone else to do it for you, than it is to follow through with it.

A construction project is never realized merely from having a set of blueprints on hand, regardless of how well prepared and elaborate it may be. Construction projects become realities only when action proceeds from the plan. And so it is with fund-raising. Working your fund-raising plan requires an on-going review of work done to date and evaluation of results achieved, always comparing them to what was planned and taking the necessary steps to stay on course. The first step of ***The System*** is to **plan your work** and **work your plan**.

CHAPTER 2

STEP 2: BELIEVE IN THE CAUSE.

Not long ago, I helped a group with a self-study project. In the midst of one of our meetings a board member suddenly burst out in a loud voice, "Do you know what's wrong with this organization?" All the people stopped and listened as he answered his own question. "Not enough of us have a fire in the belly for what we are doing!" I knew exactly what he meant. Not enough of the board members were totally committed to the mission of the organization. Not enough of them had a burning desire to see the organization succeed and fulfill its mission. Not enough of them were willing to make the personal sacrifices of time, energy, and financial support necessary at that particular time in the life of the organization. Not enough of the board members were passionate about what they were doing.

The second step of ***The System*** requires that one must believe in the cause—be completely committed to the cause—for which he or she is seeking contributions. The emphasis of this step is on the selection of the professional development staff, volunteers, and paid consultants. As will be discussed in more detail in later chapters, it also applies to presidents or executive directors and board members, all of whom play a significant role in fund-raising.

Concentrating on this step of ***The System*** goes to the very core of fund-raising because it focuses on the inner feelings and value systems of staff members—both the paid professionals and the volunteers. Most potential contributors innately sense the level of sincerity and passion of the people asking for a contribution. Although difficult to pinpoint, passion and sincerity are conveyed in our words, tone of voice, degree of enthusiasm, persistence, overall knowledge, willingness to listen and answer questions, and our general demeanor. People in sales will tell you that enthusiasm is a large part of the sale. Similarly, a potential contributor senses our passion and sincerity, or lack thereof. If a potential donor senses a lack of genuine enthusiasm or any insincerity on the part of the person asking for a contribution, any gift that may be received will most likely be of only a token nature.

Our job as fund-raisers is to create and sustain passion and enthusiasm in our contributors for our respective NFPs. When possible donors get a "fire in the belly" about a cause, they will respond. It is essential that all people associated with the fund-raising efforts of your NFP have passion, enthusiasm, and a strong belief regarding your cause, whether it relates to education, religion, medical research, the arts, ecology, outreach, safety, capital improvements, etc. That is what Step 2 of ***The System*** is about.

Selection in Small Organizations vs. Larger Organizations

Applying Step 2 has greater impact, at least on the surface, for smaller NFPs. In larger NFPs, there is usually a director of development who is experienced in most facets of fund-raising and supported by several staff who are specialists in specific funding activities—the annual fund, capital campaigns, deferred giving, etc. So, for example, when the annual fund drive is being conducted, it is easier to select staff members who are excited about annual funds and know all about them; likewise, when the funding effort is upon some other facet of fund-raising. By contrast, in smaller NFPs with only one to three people in the development office, the depth of expertise or time available from staff members to provide truly capable leadership for all the different funding efforts is not there. Some very small groups do not have even one full-time person dedicated to fund-raising.

Contrary to what most people not well acquainted with fund-raising assume, smaller organizations with fewer staff persons often need more experienced and qualified development directors because they have to know how to do it all. The development director in the large institution will have a very diversified and in-depth support staff that provides a broad range of expertise. In most instances, the smaller organizations do not have the financial resources required to employ the more qualified fund-raisers as full-time staff members. So what do they do? Where do they come up with the committed person to direct the annual drive if they do not have the person on the staff qualified to do that? Or for deferred giving? Or for special projects?

Best Use of Consultants

Experience has taught me that what works best is the combination of in-house staff, local volunteers, and, at times, outside paid consultants. Outside consultants are very commonly used on a part-time and project-specific basis, for example, when large sums are being raised, when funds are needed for unusual purposes, or for first-time funding efforts. In general, the best results are realized when professional consultants oversee the general planning process and, when needed, the training and supervision of the development team. However, the in-house staff, volunteers, officers, and board members should be the ones who actually ask for the gifts.

In general, you will raise more money and create a greater likelihood of receiving future additional gifts by having in-house staff members and volunteers asking for gifts versus using outside consultants in this role. But the staff and volunteers must be knowledgeable and trained in the techniques of asking for gifts. Larger organizations and institutions with more development staff members who have far-reaching fund-raising expertise will also occasionally find it necessary to use outside consultants, although not as frequently as the smaller ones. With any development undertaking, it is crucial that all of the people involved—including paid staff, officers, board members, volunteers, and consultants—are totally committed to the mission of the organization and truly believe in the specific causes for which funds are being sought.

How to Select the Right People

Some ask how they can be certain that the people they select are truly committed to the mission of the NFP. Unfortunately, there is no way of being absolutely certain. But some definite things can be done to enhance the selection and employment process. The following six procedures are particularly important.

First, take your time. Not taking enough time to do an appropriate search is one of the most common reasons for selecting the wrong person. Do not be hurried into making imprudent decisions. Acknowledge (or educate the impatient ones) that finding, screening, selecting, and employing high-level fund-raising personnel is a very time-consuming process. Be prepared to take the time needed to do the job right. Many NFP executives get into trouble with their governing boards because of the sloppy and lackadaisical way they went about selecting and employing people who ended up having to be dismissed.

Second, determine who will conduct the search and outline the search parameters. When hiring a director of development, the search usually should be conducted through the president or executive director's office; it should go through the development office when selecting fund-raising staff members. Determine in advance all of the details surrounding the search and employment process, and outline who will do what. Commit the employment details to writing: job description, organizational chart, expectations, advancement opportunities, evaluation procedures, salary, benefits, etc. Do not wait until you have the ideal candidate to seek approval for all of these matters. Be certain that you have the authority to employ, and on what terms, prior to initiating the search. Failure to get these details settled ahead of time can create long-lasting problems.

Third, if you are serious about raising money, employ someone with fund-raising training and experience. A common misperception among many people is that fund-raising is easy and that anyone who is friendly, well known, or has business experience can do it. A prominent Midwest symphony that has frequently achieved national recognition suffered severe financial shortfalls in the late 1990s. The symphony turned to a retired, successful CEO from the for-profit sector to raise significant amounts of money. Perceived advantages were his popularity in the city and his impressive list of contacts. Unfortunately, the symphony, several years later, is still struggling substantially. Although the retired CEO was very successful in business, he lacked adequate fund-raising experience. Fund-raising is a profession that requires specific training and expertise.

Fourth, use staff members, volunteers, officers, and board members to select and interview a short-list of candidates. Professional search firms may be more experienced and better equipped to sift through multiple applications more quickly, but locals are better qualified to select candidates that fit well into the community and mesh with other personnel already on board. Relying primarily on local people (paid staff members, community volunteers, and board members) throughout the selection and employment process will also enhance local interest in and support of the fund-raising efforts. If an organization or institution has not previously employed fund-raising personnel or does not have a development department, it may be wise to use a consultant in guiding the decision makers through the selection and employment process. The bulk of the work and all major decisions concerning the screening and employment process should, however, be made by local people.

Fifth, once you identify the candidate to whom you are seriously considering offering the position, it is essential that you follow up on references submitted by that prospective employee. Obviously, most people will only submit references they believe will say good things about them. But you can learn a great deal about the prospective employee by speaking with the references in detail. Besides verifying the accuracy of basic facts and accomplishments, you need to have the references reaffirm the positive feelings you have about the candidate as well as directly address any adverse concerns you may have. Do not ask just "yes" and "no" questions; ask open-ended questions that will lead to discussion and elaboration. For example, in referring to the candidate, you might say: "Tell me about her most impressive accomplishment." Or, "When were you most proud of him?" Or, "What was your greatest disappointment with him?" And after hearing the initial answers, probe for details. I strongly recommend following up on at least three references.

Sixth, once you have decided upon your best candidate, spend some one-on-one time with this prospective employee before extending an offer. Make certain you feel comfortable with this person, think he/she will be a good fit, and are confident in this individual's total commitment to your cause. There are many possibilities: playing golf or tennis, going out to dinner or a play, going to a concert, fishing, spending a leisurely night out, taking a walk, sitting around exchanging ideas or discussing a book both of you have recently read, or exchanging development "war stories."

Now listen up! At this point in the selection, many people make a huge mistake by employing someone about whom they feel uncertain. If you have any substantial doubts about your candidate, either rule out that person as a viable candidate or postpone making a final decision until you either eliminate or confirm your doubts. Even if you are embarrassed to change your mind at this late stage, are hard pressed to fill the position ASAP, or do not think you have the time, patience, or energy to go through this very draining selection process again, I repeat—do not employ the person if you have any genuine doubts. The later repercussions of a hurried, incorrect decision will be far more devastating than completing the selection process correctly at a later, more inconvenient date.

Be Selective When Recruiting Volunteers

It is just as important, maybe even more crucial, for volunteers to believe in the cause. After all, they serve on significant committees, represent the organization in the community, and frequently are involved in actually asking for money. Sometimes we development people are so grateful to get volunteers that we take anyone who steps forward. Or we are also concerned that we will hurt feelings if we say "no thanks" to a well-meaning but inappropriate volunteer. My very strong advice is not to get weak-kneed when it comes to rejecting volunteers who are unsuitable for the task at hand. Be selective, decisive, and diplomatic when selecting and recruiting volunteers, always making certain that they are totally devoted to the cause and will work well with the other members of your team. Also remember that it is more difficult to get rid of a volunteer who is not well suited for the work than it is to recruit one who is.

In Summary

The fund-raiser's passion, enthusiasm, and commitment for the mission of an NFP play a substantial role in fund-raising. When potential contributors sense these, they respond by wanting to help and be a part of the cause.

You may wonder why I spent so much time in a book on fund-raising discussing the details of selecting personnel. It is because Step 2 of ***The System*** emphasizes the need to know the true character and inner feelings of those who are involved with your fund-raising efforts. This step is crucial to fund-raising success, and the selection process of development personnel—paid and volunteer—is of prime significance for the realization of this step.

In this day and age, there is so much emphasis on technical skills that we tend to forget the human element of caring deeply about the mission or cause for which the money is being raised. I am not suggesting that technical knowledge and skills are not important; of course they are. But the capacity for having "a fire in the belly" for a cause and being able to inspire that passion in others are equally as important, perhaps more important. If a person is deeply committed to a specific cause or NFP, the technical skills can be learned or acquired. It is difficult to learn or acquire passion!

Step 2 of ***The System*** is to believe in the cause.

CHAPTER 3

STEP 3: THINK OF YOURSELF AS A MATCHMAKER.

I often think of a fund-raiser as matchmaker, one who matches charitable-minded people with NFPs seeking charitable contributions. There are many people who sincerely want to contribute to worthy causes and will contribute to those they are attracted to. At the same time, there are many very reputable NFPs that need financial donations. It is our job as fund-raisers to bring the two together, to "make a match." Remember, it is not always love at first sight; a good fund-raiser sometimes has to work at finessing the match between the donor and the donee. Additionally, the successful fund-raiser must continue to court the contributor after the match is made.

This is Step 3 of ***The System***—think of yourself as a matchmaker who specializes in financial courtships.

Competition for Charitable Gifts is Fierce

The need for charitable gifts is greater than ever before. Each year the number of NFPs registered with the Internal Revenue Service is increasing, as are the costs of doing business for nearly all NFPs. At the same time, many charitable organizations and institutions are finding it more difficult to raise the money needed to operate in the black. As pointed out in the Introduction, it appears that the scramble for charitable gifts will continue well into the future. That said, however, there are currently hundreds of thousands of generous people who regularly contribute to charitable causes. Their generosity spans the gamut of interests and needs. Some people give smaller amounts to several groups, and others give larger gifts to only one or two NFPs. Most would contribute to additional worthy causes, but their financial resources are limited, and they must make choices.

Individuals contribute, by far, the greatest percentage of philanthropic dollars. However, foundations, corporations, organizations, and agencies also are substantial contributors.[1] Since their financial resources are also limited, they, too, must make choices, something that fund-raisers occasionally fail to realize. Foundations and corporations usually give to several causes, and they will normally announce the specific areas of concern to which they contribute. These areas of focus usually change from time to time, generally every five to seven years. Foundations and corporations usually have a preferred format that grant proposals must adhere to, and it is extremely important that your proposal follows those guidelines specifically. Grant proposals will be discussed in detail in Chapter 9.

Know the Interests and Desires of Potential Contributors

In most instances, gifts do not just happen. Contributions are usually the result of a concentrated effort to bring together the giver and the receiver. Too often, however, the people soliciting funds think more about themselves than about the thoughts (and hearts) of their potential contributors. When that happens there is no match and, consequently, no contribution. I know only too well.

When I was president of a small college, a foundation that had given consistently to us had an end-of-the-year surplus of funds. Its' board of trustees informed me that it would consider giving the college an additional $125,000 if we submitted an acceptable proposal for a special project of our choosing. At the time, the college was in the process of developing a faculty-exchange program with colleges and universities in Eastern European countries. Our college was small, and we considered this to be a high-profile program that would give us national recognition.

Concentrating primarily on the college's agenda and paying no attention to the historical giving patterns of the foundation, we requested funding for the initial stages of this new exchange program. Given our long and friendly relationship, the foundation's consistent giving record to us, and the fact its board had contacted me suggesting the college submit a proposal, we assumed that the foundation would approve almost any project we submitted. This was not the case. The board voted against funding our proposal.

We had been unusually successful with previous grants from this foundation. Heretofore we had been careful to follow all twelve steps of

The System. But this time, we were in a hurry and too sure of ourselves, resulting in our taking shortcuts. We ignored the background and business interests of the individual board members. Most were staunch conservative business people who, at that point, had little use for or trust in the leaders of Eastern European countries. Had we followed the steps of ***The System***, our research would have shown that the board had never funded similar projects and would be unlikely to approve ours. Instead, we were so focused on our own agenda and so self-assured by our history of successes that we ignored the foundation's agenda and past giving habits.

Ironically, ***The System*** also saved us. One outcome of following ***The System*** is building the kind of rapport with contributors that assures repeat giving. After the trustees of the foundation rejected our proposal, they contacted me again and suggested that the college submit a new proposal, this time focusing on technology. Our new proposal resulted in a three-year grant for $375,000 to rebuild and reequip our outdated computer laboratory. The match was made; the foundation was interested in funding technology, and the college certainly had a need for new computers. It is interesting to note that the match was made not because of what the college did, but because of what the foundation suggested. It is important to know and pay attention to the interests and desires of your contributors.

Be Familiar with Different Terms

Prospective donors like to deal with seasoned professionals, who instill trust and confidence that their money is in good hands. Many foundations and individuals make decisions about the ability and competence of fund-raisers based on their titles and track records, level of professionalism, understanding of business terms, and use of fund-raising terminologies. As fund-raising concepts have been changing over the years, so has fund-raising terminology. Four overall titles are currently in use for people who engage in the business of raising money: fund-raiser, development officer, advancement officer, and director of external affairs.

For many years, **fund-raiser** was used for any person professionally engaged in raising money. Currently, it is used more narrowly to describe a person who raises "X" number of dollars for a specific cause in a limited time frame. For example, an educational institution needs a new piece of expensive lab equipment before starting a new program. Or it must have a certain number of new computers by a specific date in order to keep its accreditation. A small organization needs to employ a part-time office clerk. A church needs to conduct a special campaign to reduce debt or to buy the adjacent lot that has just gone on the market. A member-driven NFP needs funds to conduct an all-out membership drive to curtail operating deficits. You get the idea. These examples, and many more that you may think of, call for a specific amount of money needed by a certain date. The person responsible for executing these efforts is called a "fund-raiser." In short, a fund-raiser deals with more immediate and specific needs that have a degree of urgency to them. He or she plays an invaluable role in the funding efforts of many NFPs.

Development personnel are people who are responsible for the more long-term fund-raising efforts of an NFP. As board members and officers of NFPs increasingly faced up to the need for long-range financial well-being, they had to **develop** funding strategies that would carry their respective NFPs into the future for 10, 15, or 20+ years. As a result, those responsible for the comprehensive funding efforts began to be known as "development" personnel instead of fund-raisers. Development officers have to be fund-raisers; if they are unable to raise the money needed to underwrite today's expenses there is little reason to plan for the future. But in addition to raising money for current expenses, they have a much more sophisticated responsibility; they have to devise, initiate, and administer strategies that will assure the financial security of their NFPs for generations to come. In larger organizations, there can be a distinction between fund-raisers and development personnel. In smaller organizations the distinction between them is more blurred because of the necessity for individuals to "wear many hats." When an organization has only one staff person responsible for raising money, I strongly suggest the use of the word "development" to describe more adequately that person's broad range of responsibility. Many fund-raisers in smaller organizations aspire to become development officers in larger ones. In order for this transition to be a successful career move, the fund-raisers must have a thorough understanding of the intricacies of long-term financial security and the various kinds of fund-raising activities needed to make that security a lasting reality.

Advancement is a more recent term. At some larger institutions, the term is used for the vice-president for advancement or as the advancement officer, indicating the need to find funds and other resources to "advance" the institution.

In order to coordinate all of the resources that could be helpful in the financial matchmaking efforts, it is very common to have public relations, alumni affairs, and development departments working together under the umbrella of one office. This will usually be the advancement or development office. **External affairs** is the most recent terminology used to describe the umbrella office of several departments working together for fund-raising. The term implies reaching outside of the NFP in its search for funds.

Utilize the Efforts of the Entire Group

Regardless of what terminology is used to describe the umbrella office, the concept makes good sense. An integral part of the planning process (referred to in Chapter 1) is to find the best ways to match potential contributors to your NFP. One essential activity is to publicize your activities, accomplishments, plans, and needs. If you want to attract contributors, you must pull all the strings and use a broad range of resources to get your cause before the public. This can be done most effectively when multiple departments work together, including the development office, the public relations department, and the office for alumni relations. But smaller organizations that do not have the multiple departments should not be discouraged as they, too, can be effective in getting their needs before the public.

Here are some possible examples for use by NFPs of all sizes.

1. Direct-mail campaigns that are carefully planned and well executed. Direct-mail campaigns will almost always reap a good harvest if done in good taste, if reliable mailing lists are used (something we will talk about in Chapter 5), and if you follow up on your responses in the right way (also dealt with in Chapter 5). Successful direct-mail programs are usually administered by the development office and will reap the best results when supported by an effective public relations program and alumni participation.

2. Planned giving seminars targeted for the general public or specific audiences, either conducted by the director of development (if he/she is qualified to do so) or by an outside consultant specializing in such events. Churches, performing arts organizations, museums, and small organizations with few development staff members are excellent entities to partner with for such activities. Someone may suggest that working with other NFPs on such projects could be counterproductive because the prospective donors may be confused about whom they should contribute to. Near the end of the Introduction five fundamentals of fund-raising are outlined, and the fourth one is the necessity of teamwork, including the entire NFP sector working together. Chapter 6 deals extensively with the need to identify people who have contributed to **any** charitable cause. Working with others in creative ways will definitely benefit all organizations involved.

You could also arrange a course of study that could be approved for continuing education credits for attorneys, CPAs, estate planners, stockbrokers, and insurance agents. Many of these professionals will be eager for the opportunity of honing their planned-giving expertise and receiving professional credit. They will also be happy to learn that your organization understands the intricacies of long-term fund-raising, and they will be more likely to remember your NFP when they have clients who are undecided about where to give their money.

If you allow yourself to dream, there are many very viable ways to get your message before the public. The development office will be most successful when being supported by the public relations people and the alumni in advertising events and recruiting participants.

3. The public relations department can be extremely helpful with newsletters, news releases about every aspect of your NFP's activities, arranging speaking engagements for development staff and other appropriate personnel, arranging special events, making arrangements to attend trade shows and other events where one's "wares" can be displayed, scheduling public-service announcements through the media, arranging for special interest stories to be printed in newspapers and magazines and aired on radio and television, to mention only a few possibilities. Service clubs and various other organizations, including church groups and business associations, are always looking for good speakers. In-flight magazines placed in the seat pockets of most airplanes are another source worth exploring; they are constantly on the watch for good feature articles. Unlike paid advertising, **these are all examples of exposure that is free of charge**. These activities, however, do not just happen; they happen as the result of the hard work and coordination of many concerned people.

Usually public relations departments will have expertise in generating this kind of publicity, but they need input from development personnel in order to position the fund-raising message in the most alluring and captivating ways. In small organizations that have only a development office, the development personnel will need to take on the responsibilities of a public relations department.

4. Working through alumni to raise money is a natural. Many alumni know your programs and needs and are often excited about helping. You probably will not receive large financial contributions from alumni who have recently graduated or completed your program, but you do receive small gifts that frequently establish the early habit of contributing. Many times recently graduated alumni can help with non-monetary contributions, which are discussed in Chapters 8 and 9. Alumni serving as fund-raisers can be very useful in helping match potential contributors with those seeking contributions. In most instances, they will need the guidance of development personnel and help from public relations to have their most significant impact on the fund-raising efforts.

It is important to use all possible resources to get your name before the public, to tell them about your mission, and to let them know your needs. When you do this, it is absolutely amazing how ***The System*** will take over and make the matches for you, even when you are unaware.

Let *The System* Do Its Magic

One summer day in Kentucky, at the small church-related college where I was president, I was working in my office when my secretary interrupted to say there was a couple in her office who had stopped by to see our campus. They were farmers from Iowa who were vacationing in our part of the state and thought it would be interesting to visit our college. They did not want to be a bother, but wondered if someone could show them around. I thought that I had more pressing tasks than to spend my time meeting unscheduled sight-seeing farmers from Iowa. I telephoned the vice president for financial affairs and asked him to have a work-study student show them around.

About 30 minutes later the vice president came excitedly into my office. The two visitors were an older couple with no children, and they were trying to decide how to dispose of their estate when they died. They had read about our college, along with several others, in the national publication mailed across the country to all members of our church denomination. They had spent the past two weeks driving around the country visiting the colleges they thought they might like to leave their money to. Our college was the last one on their list to visit. Once I knew their purpose, I told them about our school, its purpose and mission.

The story has a happy ending; they included us in their estate. (I had several sleepless nights before we received the good news and kicked myself for not personally welcoming them to our school before turning them over to the financial affairs office to have a work-study student give them a tour.) They prepared a will that split the primary part of their estate into fourths. One fourth went to the college in the East that she graduated from; one fourth went to the college in Iowa he graduated from; one fourth went to their church; and the final fourth was to go to our college. We had followed ***The System***, and the match was being made without our even being aware of it.

On another occasion, I spent several hours with the chairman of our board going over plans for a complete renovation of our large reception room and identifying a prospective donor to underwrite the project. We decided upon a family to ask. I presented the proposal to a gathering of several members of the family; they appeared appreciative but were not interested at that time. I then had a second meeting with the board chairman to brainstorm and identify another prospective donor. We had barely said hello when he asked, "Would it be all right with you if I donate the funds needed to renovate the reception room?" He had been mulling over this idea since our last meeting.

In both of these instances I followed ***The System***, and ***The System*** did its job. Our story went out for prospective donors to read and hear about. The people from Iowa read about our college in an article that was prepared by our public relations director and printed in an issue of the national publication of our denomination, and the chairman of our board learned about the details of the renovation project from me when we were trying to identify a prospective donor. In both cases the match was made. Prospective donors and the college were brought together, and gifts were received.

In another example shared with me by one of my daughters, a women's shelter was desperately short of towels and linens. A volunteer devised a simple fund-raising project. She sent an e-mail to her friends, who forwarded it to their friends, inviting them as a group to attend a movie, *The Secrets of the Ya-Ya Sisterhood*, on its opening weekend at a Saturday matinee. It would give the women a chance to make new friends, watch a good movie, and contribute to a worthy cause. To "qualify" each had to bring a set of towels. The volunteer pre-arranged with the movie theater to reserve a block of seats, have special "donation" tables for the towels, and provide coupons for discounts on concession treats. The moviegoers had a good time, the movie theater was able to contribute with little effort or expense, and the shelter received over 50 sets of towels. It took the volunteer fewer than three hours to organize.

The System works! Get the word out, and matches will occur.

Learn From the Examples (Good and Bad) of Others

Because I spent a large part of my career as a parish minister, I am always curious about the successes and failures of churches. I have come to the conclusion that churches, overall, do a poor job of Step 3—being a matchmaker and getting their names and activities before the public. Although the next several paragraphs refer specifically to churches, other NFPs can learn from them. Here are some of my observations.

The large signs and bulletin boards in front of many churches include the name of the church and sometimes the head minister, but do not list popular church activities. Some do not even list the times of worship services, and letters can be small and difficult to see when driving by. The glass in enclosed bulletin boards is frequently not cleaned, and some signs that use changeable letters have old rusted letters or broken and mismatched plastic ones. Signage is often poorly lit at night.

In our technically savvy age, many churches (and other NFPs) use out-dated telephone equipment with antiquated answering machines. Informational messages are spoken too quickly, are unclear, and do not give people time to write.

Partially as the result of inadequate funds, churches spend little money on advertising, and when they do it is often dull, unimaginative, and uninspiring. In newspapers across the country, the media details scandals, but we seldom hear about the amazing stories of encouragement and inspiration that regularly come from churches that many people would find both interesting and helpful. Granted, the media often seeks scandal over inspiration, but frequently church leaders fail to publicize the inspirational news. Church leadership, however, is not totally to blame. Except for the sensational or "spicy" stories that occasionally come from the church, or the religious news that is of special national or international interest, it is common practice for the media across the country to assign new, inexperienced, or part-time reporters and ad writers to cover religious matters.

Churches are filled with successful business people, but many of them seem to regress when conducting church business. They fail to apply the savvy practices that made their businesses successful and often ignore many common "do's and don'ts" of public relations. Recently, I drove by a church close to my home. The sign in front of the parking lot said, "Due to continuing damage to our landscaping and curbing, we regrettably post our property: NO TRESPASSING. Thank you."

Following an Easter sunrise service sponsored by several churches in St. Louis County, the participating clergy huddled together and chatted, shaking one another's hands, hugging each other, patting each other on the back, and telling themselves what a meaningful service it had been. But they did not greet the worshippers, some of whom I know for a fact were looking for a new church home. It is not always that way. A monastery in St. Louis has this sign by its entrance: "All are welcome to come pray with us."

Another church in the area, which has grown by leaps and bounds, does a very good job of outreach to prospective members in their neighborhood via direct mail. Colorful, upbeat postcards are used that invite "their neighbors" to holiday services and to hear special speakers they host through the year. The church also advertises regularly via radio, TV, and newsprint; has stories about their activities on the church page; and utilizes well-known members of the church as spokespersons.

Another positive example is a church that advertised on a bulletin board of a busy highway leading to the downtown area of a vibrant Midwestern city. For one month there was only the picture of an overstuffed chair by a fireplace—with no wording. For the second month a dog was added to the picture, curled up in the chair—but still no wording. Everyday when people passed the billboard they looked for new clues that would reveal its significance. That billboard was a topic of discussion throughout the community. Finally at the beginning of the third month, when the billboard had caught the attention of many, the following words were superimposed across the picture of the dog curled up in an easy chair in front of a fireplace: "They sure know how to take care of a fella at First Lutheran Church." The church got high marks throughout the city for its creativity. It continued using billboards for another nine months and attracted a substantial number of new members.

Fund-raisers are familiar with an old cliché: "If you have *friend*-raisers you will automatically have *fund*-raisers." In other words, if you make friends and nourish those ties, you bring together those who want to give with those who want to receive. The match is made. The third step of ***The System*** is all about the necessity for fund-raisers to be matchmakers.

Nourish Matches Through An On-Going Courtship

Part of the long-range success of the matchmaking process is to nourish the matches that have already been made. Recently, a prestigious prep school in St. Louis made the mistake of not "courting" its existing matches. The school began issuing $25 tickets to students who parked in the wrong place in the school's parking lots, even if the violation occurred before or after school hours. If the student did not pay the fine within a certain number of days, a statement was sent to the parents. We can all agree it would be a hassle to have students parking in the wrong places, but more than a few students and their families concluded that the school, without giving much thought to what the reaction might be, had devised yet another way to generate additional income. Parents were irritated that the fine was more than 2.5 times the city average of $7-10, and they became frustrated that it was enforced during non-school hours.

Simultaneously, the school's development office kicked off its annual fund campaign. Tuition was expensive, and many parents were annoyed with their children and the school's policy of charging such expensive parking fines. All of this did not bode well for the annual campaign. Several parents who had contributed in prior years ended up either reducing their contributions or not contributing at all. They decided the parking fines could count as their contributions to the current annual fund campaign.

The third strike came soon after by the headmaster, who had vigorously supported the parking-fine policy. He mailed parents a very business-like letter informing them of an unexpected tuition increase for the next year. The reason given was the decline in the value of the school's investment portfolio, making it necessary to have the parents (and in some instances, grandparents) make up the shortfall. Those who were responsible for paying the increase in tuition could relate personally; they, too, were suffering from reduced values in stock portfolios and retirement accounts. Many became angry that the school viewed them as the only solution to making up the shortfall. There was nothing in the letter to suggest any sympathy, nothing to indicate that the school had done everything possible to avoid having to increase tuition, and nothing to suggest that the school and the parents would share the burden or collectively find alternative ways to address the expected deficit. There was only a business-like decision that the school needed more money and the parents would make up the difference. As you probably guessed, the level of giving decreased and goodwill was reduced.

My wife and I have four children. When they were in college, we gave financial contributions to two of the four universities they were attending, and with good reason. Two of the schools were very nurturing of parents and new students. They had several welcoming receptions, the rooms in the residence halls were clean, and we had an opportunity to meet several professors. We contributed to these two schools. The other schools did little to welcome parents or new students. The dormitory rooms were very dirty and required a lot of cleaning. My wife even called the president of one school to complain about the dirty rooms. The president explained dormitory policy, but did not apologize or offer to change the situation. We did not give to these two schools. Clearly, these schools forgot to nurture their matches.

Recently, I had dinner with a very good friend of mine who is a member and is treasurer of a relatively small church. When I asked him how things were going in the church, he became quite animated and shared a turn of events he called a miracle. The church is always on the brink of not being able to meet its expenses, he explained, but several weeks ago a complete stranger put a $10,000 check in the offering plate during Sunday worship. He had kept himself from becoming too excited until the check actually cleared the bank. I asked if he or the minister knew why this stranger to the church had been so generous. He said that he had no idea and did not think the minister did, either. I then asked him if the minister had visited this very generous contributor, and he replied that he did not think so. Finally, I asked if anyone from the church had sent a thank you letter. The answer was the same.[2] He confessed that until I mentioned it he had never thought about the importance of the minister or the treasurer making any contact with this non-member contributor. Even though the church did not know why, the match had been made—the church needed money and someone who had the money responded. But the church was doing nothing to nourish and sustain the match.

In this chapter it may appear that I am being unduly critical of NFPs (especially of churches) for their failure to practice effective means of establishing and nurturing financial courtships. My intention is not to focus attention on the institutions or their leadership, but on the need for adequate fund-raising education and training in the curriculum of seminaries and other educational institutions that prepare leaders for the NFP sector. I deal with this issue more fully in Chapter 7.

For long-term success, all levels of leadership must help make matches, get the good news out, nurture matches, and be careful not to do anything that will directly or indirectly harm the relationship. Going back to the historical origin of matchmaking, too many marriages fail because after the match is made the couple no longer concentrates on courting each other. Step 3 of ***The System*** is about being a financial matchmaker and making certain to continue to nourish those matches after they have been established.

NOTES TO CHAPTER 3

1. See note 6 to the *Introduction*.

2. Chapter 11 is devoted to the necessity for thanking contributors and the effective way to do so.

CHAPTER 4

STEP 4: CONCENTRATE ON THE NUMBER OF GIFTS INSTEAD OF THE DOLLAR AMOUNTS OF GIFTS.

For as long as I can remember, most people raising money concentrate on developing gift charts. A gift chart works this way. Based on the amount of money to be raised and the number of prospective contributors, fund-raisers predetermine specifically how many gifts are needed for what specific amounts, and then proceed to solicit those gifts. For example, if a relatively small amount of money is needed, say $10,000, you might predetermine that ten gifts of $1,000 would be practical. That is an easy calculation. But when you are raising larger amounts, perhaps $100,000 or $500,000, the calculations become more complicated.

The most common formula used in preparing gifts charts is that about 80% of all money will come from approximately 20% of the contributors.[1] There will be a small number of very large gifts at the top end; at the lower end, there will be a very substantial number of small gifts. In between, there will be many gifts of various sizes. As the gift amounts decrease, the number of gifts increases. These ratios are not fixed in concrete; they vary depending upon the campaign, the NFP, and the part of the country or world. But they usually will not vary by much.

Suppose that you want to raise $500,000 from about 750 contributors. A gift chart would look something like this.

1 gift	@	$ 50,000	=	$ 50,000
2 gifts	@	35,000	=	70,000
3 gifts	@	15,000	=	45,000
5 gifts	@	10,000	=	50,000
10 gifts	@	5,000	=	50,000
25 gifts	@	2,500	=	62,500
45 gifts	@	1,000	=	45,000

	59 gifts	@	500	=	29,500
	80 gifts	@	350	=	28,000
	120 gifts	@	250	=	30,000
	400 gifts	@	100	=	40,000
TOTALS	750 GIFTS			=	$ 500,000

The emphasis of a gift chart is on getting a specific number of gifts at predetermined dollar amounts, thus raising the dollars targeted. It is common practice to publish up-dated versions of the gift chart during the course of the financial campaign, showing which gifts have been contributed and those that are yet to be given. Step 4 of ***The System***, however, uses a different approach.

The System places the emphasis on the number of gifts to be solicited and ignores the predetermined amounts of those gifts. This, of course, is after you determine how much money is to be raised and what the money will be used for. It is my experience that when prospective donors know how much money is needed and how the money will be used, you will almost always meet or exceed your campaign goal when you concentrate on the number of gifts and not on the dollar amount of each of those gifts.

Emphasize the Number of Gifts vs. the Predetermined Amount of the Gifts

One determines the number of gifts needed to achieve a campaign goal after careful study and homework; you do not simply pull a number out of a hat. A hundred gifts for one NFP will not likely translate into the same dollar amount for a different group. In fact, those figures are likely to change within the same organization depending upon the purpose for which the money is being sought. So how does one decide upon the number of gifts that will be needed in any given campaign?

Taking into consideration the type of NFP seeking contributions and the purpose for which the money will be used, the fund-raiser will be able to determine: (1) the profile of the people who are likely to contribute, and (2) the likely average dollar amount of their gifts. It is then an easy mathematical calculation to determine the number of gifts needed. Each

NFP must do its own research prior to starting each financial campaign, projecting ahead of time how many gifts will be needed to reach the goal of that particular campaign.

I cannot emphasize too strongly that once prospective donors know the total amount needed and what the money will be used for, you will achieve the best results by emphasizing the number of contributions you are seeking rather than the dollar amounts of each contribution. Of course, if you are seeking funding for a specific project from only one donor, as was the case mentioned in the previous chapter when our college wanted to refurbish the reception room, you will mention the dollar amount. But with campaigns involving many contributors, the emphasis should be upon the number of contributions needed and not the predetermined dollar amount of each gift.

There are several reasons for this. As most experienced fund-raisers will agree, some of the largest gifts come from unexpected sources, and the people we often pin our hopes on do not contribute as we hoped or expected.

The People Who Give Often Surprise Us

In all the years I have been involved with fund-raising, my biggest surprise came on a Tuesday morning. Our church was in the midst of its yearly every-member canvass. A member of our church, a single woman who worked in a garment factory, came to my office without an appointment. As she walked into my office, I noticed she was carrying an old, wrinkled paper sack. She sat down across from me at my desk and said, "Dr. Bradshaw, I learned a long time ago that dough don't make you happy." She proceeded to open the paper sack and began pulling out little bundles of paper and money, totaling $128,000 in negotiable stocks, bonds, and cash. She put all of it on my desk, said it was for the church, and started to leave as abruptly as she had arrived. I was concerned about her welfare and questioned her about the wisdom of giving so much to the church, suggesting that she keep some for herself. She again looked at me and said, "Oh, ye of little faith!" She turned and walked out. I never would have imagined, even in my wildest dreams, that she would have been able or willing to contribute that amount of money to her church.

On another occasion, soon after I had accepted the call to become the minister of a church on the west coast, a single woman who had been a secretary for many years became ill with incurable cancer. Although she had left home soon after graduating from high school and had gone back for only an occasional visit, she decided to return to her small hometown in Kansas to die and be buried in the family cemetery plot. I stayed in touch with her by telephone. When it became obvious that she was failing more quickly than had been expected, I decided to go visit her. The costs included round-trip airfare to Kansas, a rental car for two days, and a motel room for one night. At the next meeting of the board of trustees I was chastised for spending that much money without prior approval and for not using my time in a prudent manner (I was gone for two days).

The church member who had gone back to Kansas died a few days later. We were surprised to learn that she left the church $180,000 in her will. Even her best friend, a board member who joined in reprimanding me, had no idea that her deceased friend had that much money or cared so much about her church. Neither did I. Nor did I go to see her for her money. I went because she seemed to need our support; I thought visiting her was the right thing to do. And she did not make the gift because I visited her; she signed her will before returning to Kansas. She made her contribution because she loved God and because the church had been a vital part of her life. You never know how much someone else may be able or willing to contribute.

Another time, when our church was conducting a campaign for a special-purpose fund, a naturalized citizen who had been a widow for over 20 years gave $20,000 to the church and another $5,000 to me personally. Again, based on her lifestyle and the apartment she lived in, I wondered if she could afford such gifts, and I certainly did not want to take money from her for my personal use. So I went to visit her. It turned out that unbeknownst to me or other church members, she was ill and did not have very long to live. She was grateful to the church for having assisted her and her husband when they first came to this country, and she liked my family and me. She wanted to give the money and convinced me that she could afford to do so. The church gratefully accepted her contribution, but I told her I could not accept her gift. Instead, I helped her select a different charity for the $5,000 she had wanted to give to me—an institution that helps care for retired ministers and other church workers. (In this instance, I served as a matchmaker for another institution.)

The Power of God and Intuition

Another reason I do not like to concentrate on the amount of the gifts has its roots in my background as a clergyman. I believe that the Spirit of God communicates with us and impacts our decision-making processes. If we ask for a particular-size gift rather than letting the potential contributor be responsible for making that decision, the opportunity for the Holy Spirit to influence the outcome of that decision is greatly diminished. I have found that in the long run it is better to let the donor and the Holy Spirit decide how much should be contributed, leaving any predetermined calculations by a fund-raising committee out of the picture. Obviously, not everyone believes in God or has the same belief in the Holy Spirit as I do. For these people, please let me reword this statement: let a person's intuition and conscience be the guiding forces in deciding the appropriate amount to donate.

In the spring of 2003, Rich Dozer, President of the Arizona Diamondbacks baseball team, attended the annual fund-raising breakfast for the Southwest Autism Research and Resource Center. The event was attended by 1,000 business and community leaders. Mr. Dozer was to be one of the lead contributors. Before attending he wrote a check for $100,000 and prepared a short presentation speech. However, he was so moved by the program that on the spot he wrote a second check for another $100,000, thus doubling the amount he had originally decided to donate. He discarded his prepared remarks, making an emotional appeal inspired by the spirit of the occasion. He also pledged that at the ball game that night his team members would wear special hats with the autism symbol depicting the missing information needed to develop a cure for autism and that the hats would be auctioned after the game to raise even more money for the group.[2]

One cannot predetermine how much a prospective donor will contribute, and it is a mistake to organize a fund-raising campaign based on such assumptions. Instead, one should concentrate on the number of gifts needed.

Potential contributors commonly ask how much their gifts should be. They ask this question because they earnestly are seeking some general, if not specific, guidelines. When asked I usually answer in this way. "It would be inappropriate for me to tell you how much you should contribute. You know how much we need, and you know that it will take the support of everyone involved to reach our goal. Of course, we want you to contribute as much as you can, but only you know how much you can afford to give. I feel certain that you will make the right decision." My experience has been that they usually do make the right decision.

Get First-Time Donors in the Habit of Giving

It is a known fact among fund-raisers that the most difficult gift to get from a donor is the first one. After someone makes an initial contribution, there is the likelihood that he or she will continue to contribute, and in increasing amounts. I do not worry about the dollar amount of the first gift; I just want the person to contribute that first time, knowing that other contributions will follow.

I knew a retired salesman who loved to play golf. Although he was not wealthy, his financial resources were adequate for him and his wife to live comfortably and to enjoy retirement. He gave to our college's annual drive and volunteered to help with our annual celebrity golf tournament. During a round of golf the two of us were playing one day, he told me that even though he now enjoyed making charitable contributions that had not always been the case. He never gave to his college for the first 20 years after he had graduated, even though he was frequently solicited. He became hooked after his college contacted him and told him a foundation offered the college a gift of $25,000 if it could get 250 graduates who had not previously contributed to the college to contribute within the next three months. He told me the offer was too good to pass up, and he contributed $10. He has contributed to his alma mater every year since then. Five years later he expanded his philanthropic outreach to include our college's annual fund. A few years, later he included our college, as well as his own, in his will. No one ever had to talk with him about the dollar amounts of his contributions. Once he made his first contribution he continued to contribute, and the dollar amounts took care of themselves. They continued to increase. That is the way ***The System*** works.

When one of my daughters was nine years old, she was watching a fund-raising telethon and called to contribute $1 (the contents of her piggy bank at the time). The person on the other end of the telephone asked, "Only one dollar?" embarrassing and discouraging my daughter. The telethon worker did not realize that the organization she represented could have attracted a life-longer giver. As an adult my daughter contributes on a regular basis to any number of charities, but not to that one. The important thing is not how much a gift is, but getting that first contribution. It is understandable that the volunteer answering the telephone was surprised by someone pledging only one dollar. Her focus was obviously on the dollar amounts of gifts and not on the number of people pledging. Her reaction underscores that well-intentioned volunteers or paid personnel who are untrained can be a detriment to your fund-raising efforts.

Examples from Other Groups

One of the most visible examples to the general public of Step 4 is the Kettle Drive used so successfully for decades by the Salvation Army during the Christmas season. The bell ringers serve as constant reminders of the need for donations and the invitation to contribute. In communities across the country there will usually be a total dollar amount targeted to be raised during the holiday season, but a particular amount is never suggested for individual contributions. The emphasis is upon individuals responding to the special spirit of the season by contributing the amount he or she thinks is appropriate. In some communities the members of various service clubs will take turns ringing the bells competing to see which club can "ring in" the most money. When this happens the club members are certainly more aggressive than the regular bell ringers, but even then there is no suggestion of how much those responding should contribute.

National Public Radio (NPR) stations have used the rationale of Step 4 in their fund-raising for many years. During a special-fund campaign or membership drive, the announcers will emphasize how many gifts are needed in order to reach the goal of a certain number of new pledges. They will frequently breakdown the goal into small, very realistic segments—a certain number of pledges during this morning's program, or between 1:00 and 3:00 pm, or by 5:00 pm today, etc. You will frequently hear the host say, for example, "We have received 47 calls, but still need 253 more calls by the end of this program to reach our goal of 300 new members." You will not, however, hear them say that they need to receive five more calls from people pledging $250 and 25 more for pledges of $100, and so on. They emphasize the number of pledges or new members and not the dollar amounts.

When dollar amounts are mentioned, they are in connection with incentives that contributors will receive for increasing a gift level or giving a specific amount. For example, if you increase from a "regular" to "contributing" member, let us say for $50 more, you will be awarded a dozen roses to be delivered to the person of your choice. Or if you become a "sustaining" member for $150 extra, you will get a free weekend for two at a bed and breakfast. If you are a first-time subscriber you may be given a T-shirt or ball cap. Such incentives are provided free of charge to the radio station by floral shops, bed and breakfasts, etc. These establishments receive free advertising and goodwill, as well as charitable gift deductions when filing their federal and state income taxes, the radio stations get more contributions, and the contributors are happy to donate more money because they are getting something extra. It is a win for everybody. The emphasis is on the number of gifts and not the dollar amounts.

Membership groups have found emphasizing this step to be very productive. What works well for many churches, alumni classes, service clubs, faculty, and board members is to encourage 100% of the membership to participate in the financial campaign being conducted but not to mention the amounts the gifts should be. Members are reminded of the importance of donating but appreciate not being pressured to give an amount more than they feel comfortable with. It is not uncommon for foundations and individual patrons to provide challenge or matching gifts when 100% of a particular membership group contributes. Individuals or families who are hard pressed financially can be part of a successful campaign by giving only a few dollars and not be embarrassed about the amounts of their contributions. Many times within a high school, training facility, or college, the graduating class of one year will challenge the graduating class of another year to see which group of alumni will have the greatest percentage of its members contributing. The emphasis is upon how many people contribute, not on the dollar value of their gifts.

Once a year on his radio show Rush Limbaugh helps raise money for a well-known national charity. In 2003, he received an award from the charity for the millions of dollars that have been raised through his efforts over the past seven years. Although he sends gifts of merchandise (this year T-shirts and ball caps) to people who contribute $45 or $270, he stresses the importance of receiving donations of all dollar values. He is careful to say that it is not at all necessary to contribute $45 or $270, and a very substantial number of people respond by sending contributions of only a few dollars.

With many fund-raising campaigns, especially large capital drives, it is common to solicit advanced pledges or contributions from a few people who will contribute some of the larger gifts. I recommend this practice in most instances. It challenges advanced givers to be the leaders in the campaign and to set the trend for others. If you are able to start a campaign by announcing that 30% or 35% of the total goal has already been pledged or contributed, it usually motivates others not only to contribute more money but to do so more quickly. Even when getting advanced gifts, it is important to stress the number of advanced gifts needed and not the amount you want each of those advanced contributions to be. In most instances, however, the lead donors will not be moved to contribute more at the last minute as the president of the baseball team was.

Some fund-raisers disagree with me on this point, and early in my career I followed the advice of others and asked for specific amounts of money. But experimenting on my own I concluded without question that I raised substantially more money and people felt better when I emphasized the number of gifts versus predetermined gift amounts. The true development professional must concentrate on two concerns: (1) raising the dollars currently needed and (2) providing for the long-range financial security of the organization or institution. Do not be guilty of emphasizing one at the expense of the other because both are crucial. By following ***The System*** you will raise the money needed now, and you will also have the financial support needed over the long haul.

If you are really under pressure to raise a specific amount of money ASAP or to be certain that a long-range capital campaign gets off to a good start, you may be tempted to listen to others who will assure you that you must prepare a gift chart and solicit predetermined gift amounts. Please remember what I emphasized in the Introduction: you are more likely to be successful if you remain true to all steps of ***The System*** than if you begin to pick and choose which steps of ***The System*** you will adhere to and which ones you will compromise. ***The System*** needs to be taken as a whole.

Step 4 of ***The System*** is to concentrate on the predetermined number of gifts needed to reach your campaign goal and not the dollar amount of each of those contributions. It has always been my experience that if this step is used in conjunction with all of the other steps, you will be successful in meeting both your short- and long-term fund-raising goals.

NOTES TO CHAPTER 4

1. For as long as I can remember, fund-raisers have used the 80% / 20% formula when planning financial campaigns. My experience as a fund-raiser has been that this is a sound formula that can be relied on. I was, therefore, pleased to read that "studies confirm" the relative validity of this formula. See *Giving USA 2002,* p. 70.

2. See *The Phoenix Business Journal*, April 4, 2003, p. 4.

CHAPTER 5

STEP 5: DEVELOP AND TEST YOUR MAILING LISTS.

Without question, the most prized and important possessions of fund-raisers are their mailing lists. I do not mean the lists you inherited from your predecessor, or the lists a friend shared with you, or ones you purchased. I am referring to the mailing lists that **you** have developed, tested, and know what to expect when using them. Every time I am asked to speak about fund-raising or development work, I make this point. Your mailing lists are your most important possessions regardless of the mission of your NFP or the size of your staff. This is true for a one-person operation as well as a large and diversified staff. Step 5 of ***The System*** calls for developing and testing your own mailing lists.

This chapter will cover many aspects of mailing lists: why they are important, how to use them, how to update them, how to buy them, and why not to sell them. It will also touch upon the use of computers in fund-raising.

How I Learned About Mailing Lists

When I became minister of the first church I served after seminary, I asked the Board of Deacons to help me identify the active and the inactive members of the church. We sat around a table and went through the membership list name by name (granted, the list of members, both active and inactive, was not all that lengthy). The board prepared two lists, one comprised of the people they perceived were active members and the other of the inactive members, an exercise, if you will, of separating the sheep from the goats. This way, I could better budget my time and not spend energy on inactive people who were not responsive to the mission and needs of the church. I did the same thing at the second church I served.

Then, I realized my mistake, and I emphasize mistake. It is a foolish minister who invites a committee to predetermine and identify the individuals and families who are and are not going to respond to his or her ministry. The deacons, at my request, were making their decisions based on how parishioners had responded to someone else's ministry. I was short-circuiting the effects that person-to-person relationships can have on what people think and feel, and I was taking out of the equation the power of God to inspire and influence people. A parishioner who responded favorably to a past minister may or may not respond favorably to my ministry. The important thing is how people will respond now, not how they have responded in the past.

In thinking about this, it dawned upon me that the same holds true with charitable donors. Just because people have not responded to previous requests for contributions does not mean they will continue to refuse; similarly, just because they have contributed in the past does not mean they will contribute in the future. Most NFPs and companies change over time, some more than others, and some more frequently. Leadership changes are the most common: new board members, CEOs, ministers, development officers, staff members, etc. These changes affect policy decisions, mission emphases, budget preparation, and the overall way a NFP conducts business, all of which affect how potential contributors currently feel about the NFP. This, of course, influences how much potential donors will give or if they will contribute at all. Equally as important is realizing that the thoughts, feelings, and financial situations of people change and that those changes also impact their giving habits.

Therefore, **successful** fund-raisers will periodically validate their mailing lists. They will experiment, test the waters, and determine for themselves if they can reasonably expect potential contributors to respond based on current conditions, not past circumstances.

Begin By Assuming the Best

How do they do this? First of all, begin by assuming that every person on your lists is likely to contribute. Do not determine in advance who will or will not contribute. Once I learned the lesson about not pre-determining whether a person will contribute, I began to assume I had a good chance of receiving money from every potential contributor **until I was proven wrong**. My willingness to be proven wrong was a major key to my success. I constantly reviewed and evaluated the results of all solicitations against the people on my lists. Staff members, volunteers, or I followed up with personal contacts and used questionnaires to help us understand what the people were interested in, what they liked and disliked, what their life-styles were all about, what their giving habits were, their expectations, ambitions, values, and anything else that might be helpful to learn more about them. Based on these findings, I could evaluate their potential interest in what we were doing, as well as their likelihood and ability to contribute. The key to Step 5 yielding successful results is keeping your mailing lists current. Although I was unhappy to do so, I never hesitated to remove people from my lists. I knew they could be added back at another time.

Based on my level of information, I could look at my lists and determine at any time, with a reasonable degree of accuracy, someone's likelihood of responding to a particular drive. Although evaluating and updating lists is time-consuming in the short-term, it saves time and money in the long-term. The execution of step five is an absolute must for ***The System*** to work.

Use Multiple Lists for Different Purposes

Many fund-raisers effectively use different lists depending upon the occasion or purpose of a particular drive. This is especially true with larger NFPs. For example, there may be a list for funding athletic events, one for funding scholarships, one for capital expenditures, for the annual fund, for seed money to help get new projects off the ground, for special programs, for computers, for the library, for social services, for the endowment fund, for estate planning, and on the list goes. Depending on a contributor's personal interest and financial means, the same person may be on more than one mailing list. I routinely suggest including on the mailing list for the annual fund (or by whatever name your NFP calls it) the names that are on all of your other mailing lists.

When planning a financial campaign, regardless of the dollar amount you are seeking, you need to determine which list or combination of your mailing lists to use in soliciting funds for that specific purpose. This approach will be the most likely to yield the intended results of realizing your current goal and preserving the likelihood of future contributions.

Years ago when I was the development officer at a community college, an alumnus contacted me to contribute a sizable gift to furnish a seminar center in memory of his brother, who had also attended the college. He had never contributed to our college prior to the gift in memory of his brother, so his name was not on any of our mailing lists. But I assumed he was a good prospect for future gifts and began, in what I thought was a very discreet and low-key manner, to cultivate him for future contributions. He evidently realized what I was doing and invited me to breakfast to discuss his commitment to contributing to "higher education." I was stirred and could picture the college receiving substantial financial support, both now and in the future.

He lived 75 miles away, and he was not the kind of man you would want to keep waiting. I got up very early to make certain that I would be there in plenty of time for our 7:30 a.m. breakfast. During the drive I considered various scenarios of what his intentions might be, including the possibility of a substantial contribution from his estate, which from all appearances would be quite large. I had no way of knowing what his specific plans might stipulate, but I was certain that the college was in for some big dollars. When I arrived, there was another man sitting with my prospective donor. I became excited, presuming this extra person to be the donor's attorney, CPA, or financial advisor. But much to my surprise—and disappointment—this other person was the president of a small, private, nearby college. My new-found donor explained that the small college was his primary philanthropic interest. I believed this to be his preemptive and polite way of telling me to back off and not to ask him for money. Needless to say, I felt dejected but tried to continue acting gracefully, and during breakfast learned that my new donor was an avid golfer.

I, too, love golf, and a few weeks later I invited him to play golf with me at our local country club, which was a fairly challenging Robert Trent Jones course. I am uncertain whether it was the reputation of the course or my company that enticed him to agree. After our game, we were sitting in the snack bar and I thanked him again for his very generous contribution for the seminar center. I also told him that the college wanted to show its appreciation by inviting him to play, as our guest, in our college's annual charitable golf tournament, an elaborate two-day affair that raised money for scholarships. He was delighted with the idea of playing, but insisted on paying his own way (again sending the message he did not want to be indebted).

He thoroughly enjoyed himself, and for the next three years he got his own foursome together, paid the entry fees and participated in the auction the night before the annual tournament. He also encouraged his friends and business associates to play, and he recruited some well-known former college and professional athletes and current coaches to participate. I added him to the annual fund list, and he contributed each year. Although I never asked him to contribute for anything else, he was instrumental in making our tournament a very legitimate fund-raising event, raising over $35,000 the third year of his participation. I understood him and knew what I could and could not expect of him. We had mutual respect for each other and made a good team. And that is what Step 5 is all about.

Keep Your Mailing Lists Current

It is necessary to keep your mailing lists current. We now live in an era of great mobility, and people frequently move. A move may be from one place to another in the same community or nearby, or to another state clear across the country. A move may or may not change a contributor's interests in your NFP. You want to make certain that any mail you send to contributors is actually received by them and not by others. If people moving leave a forwarding address with the post office, any first class mail you send to them will be forwarded, but only for a limited time. Any non-first class mail will only be forwarded if the recipient pays an extra fee. Furthermore, when the mail is forwarded you will have no way of knowing that they have moved. To stay current, I recommend that all mail be sent "address correction requested." By doing this, a letter will not be forwarded to a new address but will be returned to the sender with the new address noted on the item mailed, which means you will have the correct address and not have to rely upon your donors to notify you when they move. The cost for sending the items "address correction requested" is the same as a regular letter; an additional charge occurs only when an item is returned. Given that your list is a prized position, it is worth the extra money.

As mentioned earlier in this chapter, sometimes fund-raisers will remove names of prospective donors from their mailing lists because their research leads them to believe that these people will not contribute at the time. There are other circumstances that also call for names to be removed, and not removing them can result in creating hurt feelings and ill will.

Whenever donors request their names to be removed, fund-raisers should do so as quickly and with as much understanding as possible. The most frequent failure to remove names is when death occurs. A very common scenario takes place after an older person has had his or her name on a mailing list for many years. When the donor dies, the NFP, not knowing of the death, continues to send fund-raising requests. The next of kin who is receiving the mail writes to the NFP informing it of the death and requests that the name be removed from the donor-mailing list. Many times the name is not removed, and family members can continue to receive mail for several years. Obviously, this does not sit well with them.

My wife's parents died several years ago. Although she informed the NFPs of their deaths and requested their names be removed, she still receives requests for contributions addressed to them from a major evangelistic association. It would have been so appreciated by her if the association had sent her a letter of condolence, expressing its appreciation for her parents' long record of faithful support. She probably would have continued to contribute, at least on their birthdays or the anniversaries of their deaths. Instead, every time she receives one of its solicitation letters she is reminded of her parents' deaths and the apparent non-caring attitude of the evangelistic association. She continues to request that their names be removed and wonders when—or if—it will happen.

Our son is in higher education. We have always contributed to the university where he is a member of the faculty. When he moves to another institution, we give to that university and request that our names be removed from the one he left. When he moved from a major research university in Indiana it took two years for the development office to stop sending us appeal letters.

As mentioned above, when donors move it is common for them to shift their allegiance to other NFPs and to request their names be removed from the mailing lists of NFPs they have contributed to in the past. Or it may be that the donors no longer have the financial resources to continue contributing. This especially is the case with retired people who live on fixed incomes or donors who rely on returns from investments for their major contributions. NFPs need to be very sensitive to such conditions and respond with gratitude for past support and understanding of present circumstances.

In this day and age, with the technology that is available, there is little excuse for organizations and institutions of all sizes failing to keep their fund-raising mailing records up to date. Keeping your fundraising records and mailing lists current will create much good will and result in receiving more money.

Buying and Selling Mailing Lists

A frequent topic of discussion is whether or not to purchase mailing lists. Well-researched lists can be very productive tools for raising money. There are numerous and varied mailing lists on the market, and many people have an affinity for purchasing them. Mailing lists are available for purchase from a variety of sources and cover the gamut of possible interests to the fund-raiser. Lists are normally divided into two categories: by (1) interests and (2) demographic information. Lists that are sorted by interests include potential contributors who have historically given to specific purposes for which the money is to be used, such as capital expenditures, scholarships, emergencies, general budget shortfalls, challenge/matching gifts, start-up costs, etc. Lists sorted by demographics focus on personal data relating to potential contributors, such as gender, age, marital status, educational background, employment, income, religious orientation, region of the country or area of the city where they reside, etc.

For many years, I opposed the purchase of mailing lists. Looking back, I believe my decision not to purchase fund-raising mailing lists was based more on idealism than on realizing practical results. I thought it rather mercenary to purchase the names and addresses of complete strangers in hopes of getting some money from them. However, an incident took place in 1990 that changed my viewpoint about this.

A colleague of mine was the director of development at a small, church-related college that was experiencing a financial shortfall at the end of its fiscal year. The director suggested to the president that the college purchase a mailing list and send a special appeal letter to people who had never before contributed to their school. It was a year-end desperation ploy to avoid having to report a deficit in the general operating budget to its accreditation agency.

The president argued against it because the college had historically raised money from alumni, church members, foundations, and corporations. But given the desperate financial situation and fervent pleas of the development director, the president finally agreed to purchase the list and mail the letters. The total cost of purchasing the names and writing, printing, and mailing the letters was approximately $13,000. Within the first three weeks, the college received $16,000 in response to the mailing, all from donors who had never contributed to the college. Within the next week, the college wrote two charitable gift annuity contracts, one for the face amount of $10,000 and the other for the face amount of $25,000, again from donors who had not made any prior contributions to the college. And, other donations continued to be received in the coming weeks and months.

I do not know the total return from the initial $13,000 investment, but I do know that many of the new donors became repeat givers. Some also solicited contributions from their friends and business associates. The person who signed the original charitable gift annuity agreement for $25,000 made arrangements for a second gift annuity in the same amount a year later. The total return was considerable, and the college ended with a surplus in its operating budget, negating the need to report an operating deficit to its accrediting agency.

There is no guarantee that you will receive more money than you spend in buying a mailing list. It is important to do your homework on your new potential market and the company from which you buy the list. You want to make certain that you have a strong likelihood of receiving more money than you spend. Although using purchased mailing lists can be very productive for various church-related institutions (for example, colleges, social service agencies, nursing homes), purchased lists are not very effective for churches per se unless they have a very special ministry or are currently faced by a unique challenge with a lot of public appeal. Churches primarily raise money through their own members and friends rather than from the members of other churches or the public at large.

Where to Look for Mailing Lists

If you have not used mailing lists before or if you are not satisfied with the results you are getting with your current mailing lists, I suggest that you go to the *Yellow Pages* and look under the following categories: "Mailing Lists," "Mailing List Brokers," "Mailing Houses," and "Mailing Services." The categories differ, depending upon the geographic area covered by a specific *Yellow Pages* directory. There are more categories and more listings under the categories in large metropolitan areas than in small cities. Some *Yellow Pages* have no relevant listings. The most frequently found categories are "Mailing Lists" and "Mailing Services." You may find it helpful to go to a public library where *Yellow Pages* directories are available for most major metropolitan areas, or your local telephone office may have a collection of Yellow Pages from various locations. Another source worth consulting is the internet. Most companies that sell mailing lists or provide mailing services have the capacity to provide their services nationwide. I cannot remember ever using a local company for purchasing mailing lists or sending direct mail. The companies listed under each of the four *Yellow Pages* categories mentioned above offer distinct services relating to mailing lists and direct mail.

Mailing Lists. Companies found under this category are in the singular business of selling mailing lists. They do not provide printing or mailing services. They will provide the names and addresses to you or to your mailing service. Most companies prefer to do this electronically, but a printed list will be furnished if you prefer. Some companies charge more for the printed list. I suspect this will increasingly be the case.

Most companies prepare mailing lists primarily for use by commercial businesses, but the majority of them also have information about contributions to NFPs. Be certain that you deal with a company that has a source for mailing lists relating to "humanitarian and social concerns." This will be self-reported information provided by donors and is the basis for formulating most reliable mailing lists for use by NFPs.

Do your homework carefully, and be selective in deciding what list you want to purchase. Be certain that the interests and demographic profiles of the people on the lists you are purchasing coincide with your goals. You need to purchase the names and addresses of people who are known to contribute to similar purposes and in similar locations for which you are asking money.

For an additional charge, many companies will also provide the telephone numbers and e-mail addresses of those on the mailing list you are purchasing. In most instances this is an unnecessary expenditure. For direct mail, the telephone number is not necessary, and it is very unlikely that a telephone campaign will attract very many, if any, **new** donors. The use of e-mail to contact new or prospective donors will probably create more ill will than generate new contributions. People are accustomed to finding uninvited mail in their regular mailboxes. Even if their response is throwing it in the wastepaper basket without reading it, they are not **offended** by having received it. In the case of e-mail, however, people tend to feel that their privacy has been invaded when they receive uninvited requests for contributions from NFPs that they know little or nothing about, are not members of, or have not contributed to in the past. Also, there are many legitimate concerns about the wisdom of conducting financial transactions over the internet. I think it is quite possible that e-mail will, in time, be used much as regular mail is currently used in direct mail campaigns to attract new donors. But that is not the case now, and I recommend using regular mail for campaigns seeking new prospective donors.

When you purchase a mailing list, usually the price will vary depending on the number of times you contract for using the same list during the first twelve months of the contract term. Specific details will differ from one mailing-list company to the next, but it is customary to purchase a mailing list for: (1) a single mailing, (2) multiple use (usually up to three or five mailings), or (3) unlimited use. The more times you contract for using a list, the greater the cost will be. But if you plan to use the list more than once, it is **considerably less expensive** to contract for that number when the agreement is originally signed than it is to purchase the list new for each mailing.

Most prospective donors who are not acquainted with an organization or institution do not respond to the original mailing they receive, but they may respond to a subsequent request for a donation. Therefore, when an NFP has not previously used direct mail I usually recommend that the same mailing list be used for three different mailings spread over a period of three to six months. After the initial contract has expired, you should analyze the results and decide if you want to continue to use the same mailing list, to expand its scope, use a different list or a different company, or if, for now, you have enough names and do not need to purchase additional lists.

Mailing List Brokers. The end product of using a mailing list broker is the same as using a mailing list company. The difference is that the broker does all the grunt work. You tell the broker the defining characteristics and limiting factors of the mailing list you want to purchase, and for a fee the broker locates the best list for you. For the NFP that has a one-person fund-raising office or has not previously purchased mailing lists, the use of a mailing list broker may be the right choice. Finding and negotiating for the right mailing list can be very time consuming, complicated, and confusing. Previous experience makes a big difference. Many mailing list brokers will also recommend reputable printers and mailing services. Employing an experienced mailing list broker may well prove to be time saving and cost effective.

Mailing services. You will probably find the most companies listed under this category, and in all probability you will use at least one of these companies, perhaps more. Many of the entries will advertise as being a "full-service direct mail company." Their services will include: list brokering; graphic design/layout; full color printing; data processing; and complete mailing service (folding, inserting, addressing, bar coding, presorting, use of mailing permit, and depositing at the post office). Others will offer only printing or mailing services. You will discover that some companies do not really offer services; instead, they sell equipment and systems relating to mailing, such as: postage scales, postage meters, folding machines, inserting machines, sealing machines, bar code printers, and mail management systems.

One could logically assume that this is the ideal arrangement—a one-stop shop. Go to one company and get everything done from start to finish—from the selection and purchase of mailing lists to the mailing of the letters. But when you learn in depth about what services are actually offered, you will discover that very few of these companies have had experience in direct mail for NFPs, and that includes brokering for mailing lists that relate to "humanitarian and social concerns" and mailing rates for NFPs. In each *Yellow Pages* directory there will probably be very few, if any, companies listed under this category that actually qualify as a "full-service direct mail company" for the non-profit sector. Many of these companies, however, can be very helpful in providing good printing services, and some will do a creditable job of providing many legitimate mailing services. Before selecting one or more of these companies to work with, be certain to do your homework.

Mailing Houses. You will not find many *Yellow Pages* directories that contain this category. When you do run across one, you will find very few listings—frequently only one or two. Most mailing houses limit their services to those actually related to mailing, and most of them will have a good track record for the full gamut of services needed for direct mail. Usually they can provide mailing list brokering, and will have access to the mailing lists needed for not-for-profit fund-raising. It is customary for them to provide design and printing services, either in-house or "farmed out" under their supervision. And they will always provide stuffing, addressing, sorting, and mailing. "Mailing House" companies usually provide quality services, but they are few and far between and are fast becoming an endangered species. I prefer to work with a "Mailing House" company, but if you cannot find one you may want to consider a "Mailing Services" company that has recently bought or merged with a true "Mailing House" company.

Evaluation Procedures

Regardless of the mix of companies and brokers you decide to use, it is imperative that, before mailing any pieces, you have in place the mechanism for tracking and evaluating the results of your direct mail campaign. Many people spend money on direct mail but fail to spend the money for evaluating your results. Direct mail should never be thought of as a one-time shot. The purpose of direct mail is to secure information for building reliable mailing lists of your own. If you are unable to track specifically the effectiveness of your direct mail efforts, you will not be able to plan effectively for future mailings. Your goal should be increasing your return ratio—a greater percentage of people responding with contributions. As you use direct mail, you will learn what works and what does not. Direct mail is a work in progress. You will always be deciding what mailing list to use, the demographic information to focus on, the general design of letters and their envelopes, and how often and what time of year you should send direct mail solicitations based on what has happened in the past. If you do not have a thorough and practical mechanism for tracking and evaluation, you might as well not spend your time, efforts, and money on direct mail. Your return will be very limited.

Direct Mail Budgets

Your budget for direct mail will depend on such things as how many pieces you mail, how many mailing lists you purchase, how many times you use each mailing list, and the cost of design, printing, stuffing, addressing, and mailing. Other key concerns are your response ratio and average gift amounts.

When beginning to use direct mail, your budget will be an educated guess. If you do your homework carefully, the response rate for your first direct mailing will probably be not more than .3% to .5%, that is, three to five people responding for every 1000 pieces mailed. If you have good evaluation procedures in place, the response rate should creep up with each additional mailing. After three mailings you should be at a 1 % to 1.5 % response rate, or 10 to 15 people for each 1000 pieces mailed. Keep in mind that all the people responding will be added to your own mailing list, and the expectation is that they will continue to contribute in the future. Once you have your own mailing list established and tested, depending on the purpose of the campaign, you may well get a 25% to 30% response, and on the annual fund the return rate could run as high as 80%.

If your select reputable companies and brokers to work with in your direct mail efforts, the total cost of sending well designed direct mail should range between $65 to $80 per hundred pieces mailed, depending upon how many pieces are mailed and the design of the mailings. The costs of purchasing mailing lists, using brokers, and providing for all other mailing services (including design and printing) will decrease with the increase of the number of pieces being mailed. For example, it will cost considerably more per piece to mail 200 letters than to mail 2000 of the same letters.

It has been my experience that purchasing mailing lists and using direct mail to build your own mailing list pays high dividends over the long haul. Although there can never be guarantees where direct mail is concerned, the prudent use of direct mail will usually add to the bottom line. You will need to determine the practicality of using it for your NFP. I certainly recommend that you give very serious consideration to its use.

Selling Your Mailing Lists

Before leaving the subject of mailing lists, one last concern needs to be addressed. It is becoming common practice for NFPs to sell their lists to other non-profits and to for-profits. Under no circumstance should NFP fund-raisers sell their mailing lists. There are several reasons for this, some ethical and some practical.

Selling your lists is unethical. You are breaking an unwritten but sacred trust of confidentiality that exists between a donor and a donee. This is especially the case when the lists are sold to a for-profit company, such as a bank, a magazine, a credit-card company, etc. People do not contribute their money to NFPs so that the organizations and institutions can make money by selling donors' personal information to for-profits who will then inundate them with junk mail, telemarketing, and e-mails. It is also unethical to sell your list to other NFPs. The donors, not the recipients, should be the ones who decide which NFPs should and should not have their names, addresses, and other personal information. Every NFP should abide by the accepted ethical standards of professional fund-raisers (see Chapter 12 for details), and selling your mailing list is, without question, a "no-no."

There are some very practical reasons for not selling your mailing lists. One chance you take is that another NFP will be more effective than you are in soliciting a donor's contribution, resulting in your competitors ending up with all or part of the money you would have received had you not sold your mailing list. Another risk is that if your donors discover that you are selling their names to others, and frequently they do, you are very likely to lose them as contributors. That is one of those actions referred to at the end of Chapter 3 that can destroy a match that has already been established.

A good friend of mine, who happens to be a Republican, contributed to her local public television station. Several months later she began to receive letters from the Democratic National Committee soliciting contributions. It was not until the local newspaper revealed that the television station sold their fund-raising mailing list to the DMC that my friend made the connection. She has declined to make any further donations to national public radio or television.

I had a secretary who was an Episcopalian and was big on formal religious titles. One time she typed an information form for me that was returned to the seminary from which I graduated. Since I am an ordained minister and have a doctorate, she preceded my name with The Reverend Dr., which was grammatically and professionally correct. However, it is not a title commonly used. When I began to receive unsolicited catalogues and mail from banks and credit card companies using that title, I knew that the school had sold my name. Needless to say, that did not make me happy.

Fund-raisers may think that selling their mailing lists is a lucrative transaction. On the short term it may appear to be. But long term the fund-raisers and their NFPs will be the losers. Your mailing lists are your most prized professional possessions. Protect them and respect the many loyal and generous contributors who comprise them.

Use Your Computer Without Losing Your Personal Touch

Computers can be extremely useful to help search for, arrange, store, update, and sort information, which saves you time and makes it easier and quicker to arrive at appropriate decisions. E-mail is a very common way of communicating.

There are many effective software programs for development professionals to use in calculating the specifics of various charitable-giving vehicles, such as charitable remainder trusts, pooled income funds, charitable gift annuities, and charitable lead trusts. The calculations, for example, used in Chapter 8 to illustrate projected financial returns for various charitable giving vehicles were generated on the computer. I am convinced that we have seen only the "tip of the iceberg" of the role computers will play in the entire development process.

For all of the advantages of computers, there are, however, some limitations and pitfalls to guard against. For example, personal contacts are an essential component of successful fund-raising. Computers can help make those contacts more orderly and productive, but only people can establish the personal relationships that are so essential to effective fund-raising. Remember the old adage that good **friend**-raisers make good **fund**-raisers. Computers do not make friends with one's potential and current contributors. People make friends with other people through personal contacts. Computers cannot sit down and eat breakfast or play golf with potential contributors. Modern technology cannot visit a couple in their living room or around the kitchen table to learn what their primary concerns are or what they want to do with their estate. A new laptop, regardless of its enhanced memory, cannot discuss with a busy executive under what circumstances the foundation or company will consider making a charitable contribution. It is through personal contacts that you glean the information needed for building reliable mailing lists that lead to success in fund-raising. After you have gleaned that information you feed it to the computers. Computers are a great help to fund-raisers, but fund-risers must guard against becoming overly reliant on modern technology.

Several years ago, I was talking with a young minister whose church had about 200 members. We were discussing how to balance time needed for different pastoral duties, including visiting the sick. I asked him how many church members were currently in the hospital. He thought a minute, turned to his computer, opened his "hospital-call" file, and replied, "Two." Although I do not know the many different responsibilities he had, it seemed he should be able to remember such simple information without having to open a computer file.

It is crucial for the professional fund-raiser to have immediate recall of details of all kinds without having to turn to the computer in the midst of a very personal and important conversation with a potential contributor. Prior to major meetings and presentations, time should be spent in reviewing and committing to memory the significant details that may be needed. Most of us do not have photographic memories, but successful fund-raisers must balance their reliance upon computer memory with use of personal memory.

Conclusion

Step 5 of ***The System*** is to develop and test your own mailing lists. This step is a must, and used in conjunction with the other steps of ***The System***, it will reap many financial returns. If you execute step five 5 thoroughly, I predict that some day you, too, will say, "As a fund-raiser, my most prized possessions are my mailing lists."

CHAPTER 6

STEP 6: CULTIVATE KNOWN GIVERS.

A basic principle in fund-raising is that you should spend the majority of your time and energy cultivating known givers. A common mistake among new fund-raisers is to concentrate too much time and energy trying to attract first-time givers. Although it is necessary to spend some time seeking new support, under normal circumstances seasoned development personnel will spend considerably more time cultivating their current donors than trying to attract new ones. And when they are looking for new contributors, they will concentrate on finding people who are known to be charitable givers. Step 6 of ***The System*** is all about cultivating **known givers**.

This chapter focuses on three concerns: (1) the balance of time spent cultivating known givers as compared to new givers, (2) why you should concentrate on known givers, and (3) the value of asking for repeat contributions.

The Time-Balance Ratio

I suggest that about 80% percent of your time should be spent cultivating your current givers and only 20% in cultivating first-time givers. Assuming a five-day workweek (although in fund-raising 40-hour or five-day workweeks are the exception and not the rule), I recommend under normal circumstances that development personnel spend the equivalent of four days a week cultivating current contributors and one day a week seeking new donors. I am not suggesting that you devote all your time during four days only working with current contributors and one day working only with potential contributors. You might well spend part of each day in seeking new supporters for your cause. In short, what I am suggesting is that about four-fifths of your time should be spent in working with your current contributors.

Known givers fall into two categories: (1) people who previously have given to your NFP and (2) people who have given to other NFPs or causes. The most productive use of time is cultivating the known givers who have previously given to your NFP because they already believe in your cause or mission.

Some NFPs do not have a large base of known givers, perhaps because they are a new charity or institution or they are just beginning to emphasize charitable giving. For these it is necessary to go beyond their current giving base and attract other known givers. Chapter 3 offers some "match-making" ideas that should be considered for getting your message out to attract new donors.

It can be especially helpful for these groups to purchase fund-raising mailing lists (see Chapter 5). If you go this route, it is essential not to purchase just any list of known givers. You must purchase the names of known givers who have contributed specifically to purposes similar to which you are seeking contributions.

Too often, fund-raisers spin their wheels and lose valuable time by concentrating primarily on wealthy people who historically have not been supportive of charitable causes. These fund-raisers focus on the financial wealth of the non-contributors—the amount of money that they could give—and ignore that one reason they are wealthy is because they have given little or no money to charitable causes in the past and are not likely to do so in the future.

That said, it is certainly appropriate to spend some time focusing on first-time givers. There can always be a first time for a person to contribute to an NFP. And, as I pointed out in Chapter 4, once a person makes that initial contribution, he or she is likely to give again, and in increasing amounts. Nevertheless, the great majority of your time and energy should be spent on seeking contributions from known givers.

Known Givers are Different

People who consistently contribute to charitable causes are what I refer to as educated givers. They know how to give. Educated givers know how to budget so that they are able to contribute a certain amount of their income or savings to NFPs on a consistent basis. They know how to make their contributions go as far as possible. They know about matching gifts. They know about challenge grants. They know the tax advantages of contributing shares of stocks that have *appreciated* in value rather than donating cash, and in selling shares of stocks that have *depreciated* in value and giving cash. Those who are accustomed to making large contributions, say in excess of $5,000, will know about the various charitable giving vehicles they can use for making such donations (see Chapter 8).

Known givers enjoy giving, they know that charitable organizations of all kinds depend on donations for their very existence, and they know how to give. They are committed to the not-for-profit sector, and it makes good sense to turn to them.

Since known givers are educated givers, they will expect the askers to know what they are doing. It is both challenging and exciting to develop strategies with known givers. Even experienced fund-raisers will frequently have their understanding of charitable giving broadened as they work with different known givers in finding legal and ethical ways of helping them contribute as much as possible. Successful fund-raisers will be thorough in their homework prior to meeting with known givers. That is one of the necessary ingredients for being a successful fund-raiser.

Further Cultivating the People Who Have Previously Given to Your NFP

Your highest priority should be concentrating on donors who have already contributed to your NFP. A common mistake is hesitating to ask someone who has recently contributed to contribute again. Some fund-raisers argue that it is inappropriate to go to the same donors frequently, especially if they have recently responded with a large gift. I strongly disagree. Obviously, you should not ask the same person every day or two. But once you have identified someone who has given to your NFP, I recommend that you continue to go back to that contributor on a regular basis or when a special need arises.

If you have acknowledged someone's gift with appropriate thank you's (see Chapter 11) and used the money in the manner that they expected, the contributor should be happy, and you should not hesitate to ask for another contribution. In fact, most contributors will be pleased that you have asked them to consider contributing again. This is true even if they are not willing or able to contribute again at this time. If the situation is handled professionally, they will most likely assist you in developing strategies to identify other potential contributors.

I learned the value of "repeat asking" early in my career, and I have used it successfully in the years that followed. During the early years of my ministry, I served a church located in the heart of a small mid-western city. When I became the minister, the membership was declining, and the church had lost much of its zeal. People and businesses were moving to the suburbs, and families were finding churches closer to their new homes. It was hoped that a young minister could help reverse the trend.

An older member came to me with a suggestion. He believed that people would always attend a function when there was plenty of good food to eat that was free (something that largely holds true today). He proposed that we hold a church picnic with activities, games, and prizes for all ages and encourage members to bring their families, friends, and neighbors. He offered to "foot the bill" for a "barbecue with all the trimmings." Late in September, we held the picnic in the large city park after the Sunday worship service and had numerous games and contests, with ribbons and prizes for participants. It was well attended and very successful. He was proud to be the sponsor, but would not reveal how much the food had cost. He was very private about things like that, but it certainly was not pocket change.

Soon after, the Board of Deacons decided that it would be very beneficial for the church to sponsor a 15-minute television segment following the 10 p.m. Saturday news. The program would be inspirational and devotional in nature, and we would invite the viewers to attend our Sunday services and other weekly activities. The Board of Deacons (responsible for programming) took the idea to the Board of Trustees (responsible for finances). Everyone loved the idea and thought the church would reap many immediate and long-term benefits. But there was one big problem. The church just did not have the money to underwrite this new venture. However, if the minister could come up with the additional funds required, the members of both boards were certain that the proposed program would be very well received by our church members and the community at large. Hence, it became my responsibility to raise the additional money needed.

I went through our entire church membership list, considering each person whom I could possibly ask for the additional funds. I came up with three names: the man who had recently sponsored the church picnic and two I did not know well. At first, I hesitated to go back to the sponsor of the church picnic. I thought that it was not fair to ask him for the additional financial support needed for the television program so soon after he had underwritten the picnic. I decided not to ask him for the money, but to turn to him for a different kind of help. I knew him better than the other two men, and I thought he could assist by encouraging them to contribute the additional funds needed. When I asked him how I might best approach the other two people it did not occur to me that he would be interested in giving another large donation so soon. But he immediately responded by saying that he wanted to pay for the television program for the first six months, and if the program went well we could consider going to the other two people for additional support.

During my tenure in this church he made many contributions and took pleasure in being a part of re-building our church. He truly enjoyed using his money to help make good things happen. Looking back on my decision, it was right that I went to him for help with the TV program. I believe that he would have had his feelings hurt had I gone to someone else first. And it was right that I continued to go back to him time and again—when the pipe organ needed to be rebuilt, to purchase one quarter of a city block for parking purposes, when we wanted to pay off the balance of the mortgage on our education wing long before it was due, to mention only a few. He did not always underwrite the projects himself, but he always helped the church find a way to do it—by an initial large gift, a matching gift, a challenge grant, contacting other individuals to join him in "priming the pump," or by referring me to other people. I learned from others that he did the same for many organizations in the community. He stayed out of the limelight, thoroughly enjoying making good things happen by working quietly in the background.

One very significant result of this man's fund-raising efforts was the influence he had on others. He helped people see the importance of taking their giving to the next level; most heavy hitters in the philanthropic armies throughout this country have worked their way up little by little to the top echelon of donors. He helped leaders throughout the community find realistic and creative ways to attract contributions for their respective NFPs. He also helped educate donors about the various sophisticated giving vehicles they could use in making their charitable contributions go as far as possible.

When fund-raisers concentrate their efforts on known givers, they have the best prospects for raising the dollars needed to meet current expenses and to assure long-term financial security.

Conclusion

Step 6 of ***The System*** is to cultivate known givers. First, concentrate on people who have already given to your NFP. Then look for people who have contributed to other NFPs that have similar mission statements to yours or who have contributed for the same purposes for which you are seeking money (e.g., scholarships, annual fund, capital expenditures, etc.). Finally, spend some of your time trying to get those people who have never engaged in charitable giving to contribute to your cause or to some charitable endeavor in the community.

CHAPTER 7

STEP 7: ASK TO RECEIVE.

When I was the senior minister of a large metropolitan church on the West Coast, I always read the Sunday newspaper before church to make certain that there was not an item that people might expect me to know about or refer to during the service. One Sunday, the lead story was about a six-figure contribution to the local children's hospital. The donors were the chairman of the board of trustees of the church I served and his wife.

Following the morning service, I talked with this chairman, as I did most Sundays, and I commended him for making such a magnificent gift. I also asked him why he had not made a sizable contribution to our church. He was quick to answer. "You didn't ask me." I responded, "But you knew our church needed it." And he said, "You didn't ask me, and they did."

He was right! I had not asked him. But I certainly did ask him soon after that, and he responded with a ten-figure gift, as he did each of the next four times I asked him. Step 7 of ***The System*** stresses the importance of actually asking for a contribution.

This chapter is about asking: its importance, different ways to ask for money, and asking in ways that do not offend. There is also a special segment for churches.

Ask and You Shall Receive

Most people are familiar with the Bible verse that says, "Ask and you shall receive." It does not say, "Hope and you shall receive," or "Inform and you shall receive." Too often, fund-raisers assume that people will make a contribution because they know of a need or because you have told them of your needs. This is not usually the case, as witnessed by the story about the chairman of the board of trustees. The chairman knew of our needs. He had studied our weekly finance reports, chaired meetings discussing how to fund our $52,000 weekly budget, and had even suggested asking some of the more affluent church members for special contributions. Yet, he did not respond until personally asked!

I have had numerous fund-raisers tell me that when they realized the importance of actually asking for a gift it made a huge difference in their careers. Some of them told me that for years they assumed they *were asking*, but then realized that they were only *talking* about need, mission, opportunity, and responsibility. Talking is not enough! Asking really does make a difference![1]

Design Your Activities Around Asking

All training classes for salespersons stress the necessity for "asking for the sale" rather than just talking about the product. The corollary in fund-raising is "asking for the gift." Successful fund-raisers have learned that it is necessary to ask in order to receive. There are many ways to ask. You can ask by letter, newsletter, telephone, radio, and television. You can also ask in person—one-on-one, in a small group, or before a mass meeting. Whatever your method(s), it is crucial that you are willing to ask.

I often hear people—especially volunteers—say they do not want to ask their friends for money. Would they rather ask their enemies? If a person really believes in the cause (Step 2), he or she should have no trouble asking anybody—friend, neighbor, business associate, golfing partner, family member, whomever—for a contribution. If we knew about a particularly attractive investment with a high rate of return and little risk, most of us would gladly share that information with friends and associates, who would appreciate being informed. Or if we knew about a really good business deal, an honest and ethical way to turn a profit, most of us would share that information. Likewise, it makes sense to share good contribution possibilities with our friends. Most people have a limited number of charitable dollars that they are able (or willing) to contribute. They choose carefully and appreciate learning about worthy, well-run NFPs that are in need of money from a source they trust.

The successful fund-raiser needs to **ask** people to give; do not assume they will contribute just by being informed. Those who ask are much more likely to receive.

A very good college friend of mine has kept me informed through the years about an NFP he founded in Washington, DC. I knew that it was a very worthy cause and was always in need of money. Yet, I did not contribute. One time when visiting DC, my friend walked me around the neighborhood his organization served, and he showed me a building he hoped to buy and renovate. His fund-raising plan called for raising the money with major grants from foundations and corporations, supplemented with gifts of all sizes from individuals. Once again, I did not contribute. After all, I had my own church that needed money, as well as other organizations closer to where I lived.

Through the years, we got together, played golf, and shared experiences. During one of our recent outings, he not only shared his need for contributions, he also asked me to contribute. While I did not contribute at that time, I did a few months later. Like the chairman of our board of trustees, even though I was aware of the need, I would not have contributed had my friend not asked me.

Asking does make a difference!

Different Ways to Ask for Money

Different people ask in different ways. The key is to ask in ways that will motivate your target audiences to respond. A number of years ago, I was asked to preach at an African American church in a small city with several colleges. Because many of the members worked on the campuses and had to be at work by 8 a.m., the service started at 6:30 a.m. It was August, and it was hot even at that early hour.

After I preached, the minister made references to how hot it was, and went on to suggest that "it is really going to be hot some day" for those who failed to fulfill their Christian responsibilities. He then asked for the offering. After the offering was received, there was a vocal solo, during which time the minister counted the offering. After the solo, he said that he regretted having "to call upon the members again," but the first offering was not sufficient. He called for a second offering. After the second offering, there was another solo, and the minister counted the money. He said it was necessary "to call upon the members yet another time." After the third offering there was another solo, and the minister again counted the receipts. This time he smiled and said this offering would be adequate. He proceeded to put the offering on the altar in the front of the church sanctuary where all the worshippers could see the money, and he then offered a prayer of blessing and thanksgiving. He concluded this portion of the service by thanking the congregation for their sacrifices.

Contrast that service with the way I asked for an offering during a very formal Christmas Eve midnight candlelight service broadcasted on a relatively powerful radio station that carried about 300 miles in all directions. The sanctuary was decorated with large cedar wreaths, and the scent of the cedar reached our gothic ceiling. The candles created a soft light, and the choir and clergy wore festive robes. An orchestra accompanied the choir, and trumpets led the congregation in singing carols.

Although the radio could not capture the physical beauty of the occasion, the radio waves seemed to transmit the special spirit of this particular service. At the appropriate time I spoke very briefly about the privilege and opportunity of giving a portion of our earthly wealth back to God to be used by the church in its ministry. I suggested that at a time of year when we are so immersed in giving presents to one another, it seemed especially appropriate to include Jesus, whose birthday we were celebrating, and the church in our giving. Although very low key, make no doubt about it—I asked people to contribute. The next week the church received a cashier's check for $125,000 from a non-member of the church who had tuned into the service while he was driving home for his annual Christmas visit to see his parents. In my wildest imagination I never dreamed of receiving a contribution of that magnitude from that service. Asking made the difference!

The minister of the church in the college town and I asked for money in very different ways and under very different circumstances. But we both asked, and both of our churches received. Do not hesitate to ask.

Asking Without Apology

Robert Schuller, founder and minister of the well-known Crystal Cathedral in Garden Grove, California, built his ministry from the beginning by dreaming big and raising the money to support his ideas. A few years ago during a Sunday worship service he said, "I will not be intimidated by people who say that I am asking for money again. You bet I am!"[2] There were many times that his dreams initially appeared to stretch far beyond his congregation's capacity to pay. But time and again he asked, and he received. Having the money to fund his "bigger-than-life" dreams has set him apart from many of his peers.

Be Careful How You Ask

It is important to ask in a manner that does not offend your prospective donors. This can happen in different ways. It is impossible to please all people, but you need to be cautious about mailing literature that will not be well received by your target audience. A small struggling organization that sends a very elaborate multi-colored brochure on slick paper may cause its contributors to wonder if their money is being well used or misspent on fancy publications. On the other hand, a single color letter on lightweight paper with no graphics may be just as out of place for a prestigious university or hospital. Give a lot of thought to the ultimate purpose of your mailings and to whom they are addressed.

When asking by mail, be certain to use the correct postage. It is a real "turn off" to receive a "Postage Due" appeal letter. Postal rules and rates change frequently. What was adequate postage the last time you mailed a major appeal many not be sufficient now. I especially caution about unusual sizes and shapes; both larger- and smaller-than-usual letters or packets may cost extra to mail. Using heavier paper than usual or inserting a pledge card may increase the weight enough to require additional postage. Bulk mailing rates also are different from regular mailing rates. Sorting your own mail and bundling according to zip codes makes a difference. When mailing any kind of an appeal that is out of the ordinary, I caution about using your own postage scales. Be safe—always check at the post office to make certain that you have the correct postage.

You want to make it as easy as possible for people to respond to your requests. I recommend including a postage-paid reply envelope with **all** requests for funds, regardless of the size or mission of the NFP. Sometimes donors will put off mailing a response because they do not have postage stamps readily available. Other people think that if they are sending a contribution the least the NFP can do is to pay the postage. (Those who want to pay the postage will just put a stamp on the envelope.)

When to Stop Asking

Some organizations make the mistake of sending repeated mailings to people whose intention may have been to give a one-time contribution. This happens most frequently when a memorial contribution is sent in lieu of flowers. It is common for the family of a deceased person to request that a contribution be sent to a particular NFP in lieu of flowers. The donor makes a donation out of respect to the deceased and not because he or she is especially attracted to the NFP. While I generally recommend that anyone who contributes to a NFP should be considered a prospect for future contributions, when it is obvious that a one-time gift is the intent of the donor, a gracious thank-you letter should be sent, and the person should not be added to one of your fund-raising mailing lists. (Thank you's will be discussed in detail in Chapter 11.)

One of the most important things in asking is to convey the impression that you are genuinely concerned about the welfare of the donor. Use your discretion when talking with different people. You do not want to come across as the stereotypical used-car salesman who may not have the best interests of contributors in mind.

A Special Section for Churches

There are several reasons I have included this special section for churches. One is because as an ordained minister I have an understanding of the obstacles that my peers face in performing their ministerial responsibilities. The great majority of religious leaders are not particularly adept at raising money, although their respective ministries are largely dependent on charitable contributions for their existence. Their seminary training rarely includes fund-raising. Hopefully this book will be of help to them in raising money.

Another reason lies in our country's Judeo-Christian roots. Our churches and synagogues have a long history of playing a predominate role in our daily lives. I believe that it is crucial for the churches and synagogues of the twenty-first century to have the financial resources necessary to continue making a positive impact on all levels of our thinking.

There is yet another reason for my emphasis on the importance of religious leaders being good fund-raisers. It is difficult to get exact figures because churches are not required to register with or report to the IRS, and some religious organizations decline to participate in financial-related surveys. Even so, available statistics indicate that between 60% and 70% of all households in the Untied States contribute to local religious congregations, their denominations, and related activities, including evangelistic associations, religious broadcasting and publishing companies, summer youth camps, and interfaith councils. This does not include, however, the contributions to other religious-related organizations and institutions, such as colleges and universities, hospitals, welfare agencies, homes for children, nursing and retirement facilities for the aged and infirmed, shelters/soup kitchens, day care centers (children and adults), and Bible societies.[3]

Of the total $212 billion contributed to all NFPs in 2001, $80.96 billion (nearly 40% of the $212 billion) went to religious congregations and related organizations. This is more than 2 1/2 times the amount contributed to education, the sector that received the second biggest amount; 4 times what was contributed to human services; almost 4 1/2 times more than to health, including hospitals; and better than 3 times the total amount contributed to all foundations. In 2002, giving to religious organizations increased to $82.83 billion and estimates for 2003 come in at $86.39 billion, an increase over a two-year span of 6.7%. No other not-for-profit sectors have realized increases of such gigantic proportions, and many sectors have seen decreases in the contributions received.[4] Whatever the total amount contributed to religion in America, both directly and indirectly, these statistics indicate a very substantial commitment by the American populace to the importance of religion in the United States.

The churches I served as a parish minister ran the gamut of educational/vocational backgrounds, social and economic status, number of members, and variety of locations. Our denomination, unlike more conservative ones, does not stress tithing or the importance of personal financial sacrifice in order to be able to give more money to the church. Nevertheless, each church I served prospered financially and expanded its ministries. Depending upon the church, we renovated and enlarged physical structures, raised funds for deferred maintenance, and purchased additional property.

Members began putting a higher priority to the dollars they offered to the church and spent less on other things so they could give more to the church. And they noted that they respected the minister for his role in helping the congregation in understanding and practicing good stewardship.

There are three things that helped me. Depending upon your situation, they could help you, too. They are: (1) taking a lead role in all financial matters, (2) making offerings an integral part of my worship services, and (3) becoming comfortable asking for money.

1. Take a Lead Role in Finances. I always took a lead role in all financial matters, from preparing budgets, to planning and executing financial drives, to asking for and receiving offerings in worship services. Some ministers feel uncomfortable and not well qualified to deal with financial matters, while others suggest that it is theologically inappropriate for members of the clergy to be concerned about money. They delegate the responsibility of asking for money during worship to non-clergy persons and participate little (or not at all) in the annual fund campaign (by whatever name it is called), leaving that task to the lay people. In some churches clergy leave all financial matters, including preparing the budget, to lay members.

The active participation of lay people is crucial. But good stewardship is a theological matter that deserves the attention, leadership, and participation of the professional clergy. It has long been my observation that churches—entire denominations—experience financial problems when their clergy fail to take a lead role in financial matters, thereby downplaying the importance and theological significance of money.

To discuss Jewish and Christian stewardship—their theologies, histories, and practices—would be a book in itself, and there are many good references already available. It is sufficient for our purposes here just to point out that the giving of money or other forms of personal wealth for religious purposes has a well-grounded biblical history, and the giving, receiving, and blessing of such offerings during worship have long been considered an integral part of both Judaism and Christianity.[5]

2. Make Offering an Integral Part of the Service. Worshippers presenting their offerings and the officiating clergy blessing those offerings are a legitimate and important part of worship. It is all about offering a part of ourselves—the results of our time, talents, and efforts, as well as in some cases, of our inheritance—to the Glory of God. It is a way of worshipping God the Creator; a way of acknowledging that He is the Creator and we are the creatures; a way of acknowledging that everything we have and own really belongs to the Creator, and we are only acting as temporary stewards; a way of using some of what He has given us to be stewards over to manifest in our daily lives some of the core purposes for our creation and existence.

Asking for, receiving, and blessing the financial offering can be a rewarding and inspirational part of congregational worship. Many church members have told me that the offertory is one of the most meaningful segments of the worship service. It is common for parents to teach their children from an early age to save some of their money for the church and to place their offering in the offering plates themselves.

In my opinion, it is not only appropriate for religious leaders to ask for money during formal worship services, it is inappropriate not to do so.

3. Get Comfortable About Asking. I am convinced that many ministers feel uncomfortable about asking for money because they do not know *how to ask*, especially during a formal worship service. Most of our seminaries are remiss in not including the theology of receiving an offering and the practical business of asking for the offering as an integral part of their curriculum pertaining to worship and church administration. Denominations should do everything possible to help their ministers develop a better understanding of church finances and provide seminars and other training opportunities on how to ask for financial support.

It is important to stress to church members the biblical, historical, and theological significance of stewardship. When church members truly understand the historical, theological, and practical connection of money with religion, most respond enthusiastically and are happy to serve God financially by giving more money to their church (or synagogue or temple or mosque).

Ministers and other religious leaders should feel comfortable about asking for money. Unfortunately, most lay people perceive ministers and rabbis as not being very astute about finances. But when religious leaders emerge as strong leaders in financial matters as well, they are highly *respected* by their parishioners.

I believe that it is absolutely crucial for the churches and synagogues of the twenty-first century to have the financial resources necessary to continue to make a positive impact in our lives. By increasing their ability to ask for financial support, they will be able to raise the funding required for being increasingly influential in today's society. One cannot help remembering that Jesus in his most famous prayer called for having life "on earth as it is in heaven." It seems to me that today's churches and synagogues and their ministers and rabbis have a clear-cut responsibility to be especially attuned to the theology of stewardship—including the why's and how's of asking for money.

Conclusion

Step 7 of ***The System*** emphasizes that the fund-raiser must ask in order to receive. Many letters, brochures, and pledge cards talk about mission and need, but fail to ask for financial contributions. Do not assume that merely describing the need will secure a contribution. The opening story in this chapter about the chairman of the board of trustees demonstrates that whoever asks is most likely to receive. Had my good friend in Washington not actually asked me for a contribution, I would not have given. Had the minister in the college town not continued to ask, he would not have obtained his financial goal for that Sunday. Had I not asked for financial gifts during the Christmas Eve service, the church would not have received a six figure offering from a complete stranger who was listening over the radio.

If you expect to receive, be certain to ask. It is not enough just to inform people of your mission and need. It is essential to ask, and that is what Step 7 is all about.

NOTES TO CHAPTER 7

1. *Giving USA 2002,* p. 70, near the end of the section entitled "Giving by Individuals," reports the following: "Donors say the most important factor affecting their contributions is that someone asks."

2. January 16, 1994, 8:45 am on TV Channel 3, St. Louis, MO.

3. In 2002 it was estimated that there are 349,506 local church congregations in the United States, plus 2,900 synagogues and 1,200 mosques, for a total of 353,506. The figures for churches come from 87 denominations or religious bodies with 200 or more individual churches; for synagogues from the United Jewish Communities; and for mosques from the Council of American Islamic Relations. These figures are constantly changing. I suspect that there are more than 353,506 local congregations due to the hesitancy of some churches to respond to the surveys and to report statistics. Also, more new churches are being organized than existing churches are being disbanded. For details, see *The New Nonprofit Almanac and Desk Reference: The Essential Facts and Figures for Managers, Researchers, and Volunteers*, a joint project by Independent Sector and the Urban Institute, published by Jossey-Bass, 2002, pp. 10-11; *Giving USA 2002,* pp. 60, 98; and *Giving USA 2003,* pp. 106-107.

4. *The New Nonprofit Almanac and Desk Reference: The Essential Facts and Figures for Managers, Researchers, and Volunteers*, a joint project by Independent Sector and the Urban Institute, published by Jossey-Bass, 2002, pp. xxxvi, 1-11, 109, 221; *Giving USA 2002,* especially pp. 6, 8-9, 11,16-19, 33, 60, 70, 98-103; various reports from Independent Sector that can be accessed on line at www.independentsector.org; *Official Fundraising Almanac*, by Jerold Panas, Pluribus Press, p. 273; *Giving USA 2003,* especially pp. 6-7, 10-11, 14-15, 28-29, 106-112; and *Giving USA 2004*, especially pp. 6-10, 48, 53, 94-105.

5. I am aware that most synagogues in the United States today are supported by dues and that receiving a monetary offering during a Jewish worship service currently is seldom practiced. I have emphasized Christianity and Judaism because of the historical connections these two religions have with the United States, a connection not shared by most other religions that are also currently practiced in this country. The main purpose of this book, however, is not to discuss religious history or to debate theology, but to put forth a system that will help NFPs raise money. Step 7 emphasizes the need to ask, and this section of the book points to the importance of all religious leaders being willing and knowing how to ask for money.

CHAPTER 8

STEP 8: ENCOURAGE USING ASSORTED GIVING VEHICLES AND GIFTS.

Make it easy! The name of the game in receiving contributions is to make it easy for your donors and give them the advantage of options. By offering and accepting a variety of giving vehicles, you will increase your donations and provide added value to your contributors

Step 8 of ***The System*** is to encourage using assorted giving vehicles and gifts. The "sky's the limit" with this step. Regardless of the size or mission of your NFP, in nearly all situations you will greatly increase your contributions by promoting and nurturing a variety of giving vehicles. Additionally, your donors will be happy and will contribute again and again.

Many smaller NFPs, including churches and synagogues, assume that most of the giving vehicles discussed in this chapter are too complex for them to use. Such a thought is a mistake that can result in your losing untold charitable gifts. It is not as difficult as many people assume to introduce your organization to using a variety of giving vehicles, and it is easier than most people believe to make the necessary arrangement for receiving contributions via most of these giving vehicles.

This chapter deals with the difference between present and deferred gifts, identifies eight giving vehicles and discusses seven of them, and talks about the merits of non-monetary gifts.

Two Classifications of Gifts—Present and Deferred

There are two basic classifications of charitable gifts: (1) **present** or **outright** gifts (the donor immediately transfers *possession* and *use* of the gift to the donee) and (2) *deferred* gifts (the unconditional commitment to make a gift is executed now but the total possession and use of the gift by the donee is deferred to sometime in the future).

Many variables must be considered in using different giving vehicles. These variables include but are not limited to: state and federal laws and regulations, actuary tables, policies by regulating boards or trustees, type of charity receiving the contribution, age(s) of donor(s), the health of the donor, needs of other family members, the income of the donor the year a charitable gift is being made, net worth of donor and other family members, tax bracket of donor, capital gains tax implications, giving history of donor, charitable giving objectives of the donor, and on the list goes. It is vitally important to understand the variables that can benefit or adversely impact the donor and the NFP. A knowledgeable professional (you or someone else) definitely needs to be involved in determining what giving vehicle should be used in each individual case.

Tax implications for the donor are the biggest concern, primarily when and how much of a charitable deduction will be realized when making a charitable contribution. Three taxes must be taken into consideration: income taxes, estate taxes, and federal gift taxes. Many people lump all charities together by referring in general to charitable organizations, but the federal government makes a clear distinction between various kinds of charities. For example, there are religious organizations, educational institutions, service organizations, hospitals, fraternal societies, etc. Gifts to some charitable organizations may qualify for one type of tax deduction, and a contribution to another will not. Or gifts to some may qualify for a maximum deduction while gifts to another will yield a lesser tax deduction.

Although most donors contribute because they believe in the mission of the NFP, they also want to contribute in ways that maximize the tax benefits allowed by law. In fact, when donors become fully informed about the tax benefits of an anticipated gift, they often contribute more than originally planned. But there are far too many cases of people believing that their donation will qualify for one type of tax deduction only to find after it is too late to rectify the situation that it did not. No reputable fund-raiser wants this to happen. When considering the use of any of the many giving vehicles that can be used in soliciting and receiving charitable gifts, guesswork, assumptions, and wishful thinking absolutely must not be allowed to influence one's decisions. Professional counsel is crucial and readily available.

It is essential to work with donors and their professional advisors, providing them with precise information. That is the only way that they can make informed decisions. And that is the way you keep donors and their families happy.

Eight Popular Giving Vehicles

There are eight popular giving vehicles or legal instruments for giving and receiving charitable contributions. They are: (1) credit/debit cards, (2) wills, (3) charitable remainder trusts: annuity and unitrusts, (4) pooled income funds, (5) charitable gift annuities, (6) deferred payment charitable gift annuities, (7) charitable lead trusts, and (8) foundation grants. Foundation grants will be discussed in Chapter 9.

It is important that NFPs be fully knowledgeable about the different ways of giving and receiving contributions, prepared to educate donors about them, and ready to receive such contributions. For readers who are not acquainted with these various giving vehicles, I have included a thumbnail sketch of each. Please remember, however, that this book is not meant to be a technical guide that explains the intricacies of each giving vehicle.[1]

1. **Credit/Debit Cards** have revolutionized the way people donate money. Although it takes a little more time initially to arrange for processing credit cards, the long-term benefits actually save time. Credit cards can be used to give **outright** and **deferred** gifts.

Donors may make a single contribution or arrange for weekly, monthly, quarterly or annual contributions to continue for a specific period of time or until they cancel their respective authorizations. Once the initial authorizations are in place, the donors and their respective NFPs have no further work outside of bookkeeping. The transactions are processed electronically, and donations are automatically credited to the bank accounts of the NFPs at the intervals specified, and the charges appear on the donors' monthly statements from their respective bank card companies.

The same procedures used for processing credit cards are used with debit cards; the only difference is that the donations will be electronically debited from the donors' designated bank accounts rather than receiving statements from their respective bank card companies that will need to be paid.

Regardless of the size of the NFP, it is relatively easy to accept credit card and debit card contributions. Arrangements are made through a bank or major credit card company, and a small percentage of the total contributions received via credit/debit cards will be charged as a handling fee by the entities processing the plastic-card contributions. The percentage figure can vary greatly from one company or bank to another, depending upon the number of transactions processed and the average amount of those transactions (the greater the volume the less the charge). Most credit card companies and especially banks will negotiate rates, so shop and bargain for the best deal you can get. Many companies will not give you the lowest rate on their first (or even second or third) offer. It is important to "hang tough" on your percentage negotiations. You will probably have a better chance of getting a lower percentage after using credit/bank cards for a period of time, say for a year. Remember Step 7—you have to ask to receive!

No matter whom you select, nearly all transactions are now processed electronically, and new accounts are required to install an electronic processing apparatus to their telephones. The company you select will help make the necessary arrangements. Some up-front costs will usually be involved, but they will pale in comparison to the benefits.

Institutional leaders who fail to recognize that the plastic card is a valid and acceptable substitute for money are living in the past. On-line banking and consolidated bill paying via credit/debit cards are very popular ways of doing business in today's world. Many people already pay monthly commitments and insurance by direct authorization, as well as receiving regular payments, such as social security, that way. All NFPs should make it possible for their members and friends who so desire to make their charitable contributions by electronic means. Not only will the NFPs receive more money, the contributions will be received on a more regular basis, especially during vacation seasons when people are away from home and not focusing on their charitable-giving commitments.

A special note to churches. Making one's offerings via credit cards received a negative reaction from most churches when the idea was first introduced over thirty years ago. There were primarily two reasons for this. First, the entire process seemed too cumbersome and impractical to be used during a worship service.[2] But there was another reason. Putting one's worship offering "on the tab" seemed irreverent, maybe even blasphemous. Today, credit/debit cards are easy to use and are universally considered as being the same as money. Many churches receive contributions and offerings via plastic cards. It is common practice for churches to provide special pew cards to be placed in the offering plates during worship authorizing a charge against one's credit/debit card. The pew cards have appropriate printed messages indicating that they represent the worshippers' sacrificial offerings and are dedicated or consecrated along with the other forms of gifts being offered. Some people make arrangements for credit/debit card authorizations through the church office but will use the pew cards to help them feel a sense of participation during worship, rather than having offering plates pass them by and placing nothing in them.

I strongly recommend that churches consider receiving worship offerings and other contributions via credit and debit cards.

2. The will, the giving vehicle most readily recognized and understood by the public, is a legal instrument stipulating how your assets are to be disposed of at the time of your death. A will may stipulate that **outright** gifts are made to people or other entities or that more complicated ways of distributing one's assets are used, including the formation of trusts and other instruments of **deferred** giving. There are a number of irrevocable life income plans that retain an income for the donor or others, while allowing the donor to claim a charitable deduction for a part of the value of the gift. Some are considered to be a trust agreement while others are considered to be a contractual relationship between the donor and the charity involved. Each has specific requirements, and each has different tax implications.

3. Charitable remainder trusts fall into two categories, the charitable remainder *annuity trust* and the charitable remainder *unitrust*. A charitable remainder trust, the instrument used most frequently in **deferred** giving, is a trust established by the donor that transfers assets that provide income for one or more beneficiaries (usually the donor and family members) for as long as the beneficiaries live or for a term not to exceed 20 years. When the beneficiary(s) dies or the term of the trust expires, the remainder of the assets goes to a qualified charity. Hence, the trust gets its name from the concept that the *remainder* is being donated to a charitable organization.

The only difference between the charitable remainder annuity trust and the charitable remainder unitrust is the way that the distributions to the beneficiaries are determined. With the annuity trust, the amount of distribution or the income to the beneficiary(s) is a *sum certain*—a fixed amount, not less than 5% of the initial value of the trust, that will remain the same for the life of the trust. With the unitrust, the amount of distribution is a *fixed percentage*, not less than 5% of the net fair market value of the trust's assets as valued on an annual basis; hence, the percentage will not change but the dollar amounts of distribution will vary from year to year depending upon the net fair market value of the trust each year. Although the annuity trust and the unitrust are similar in nature, each is subject to separate tax rules and regulations.

4. The charitable lead trust is a very attractive giving vehicle, and works exactly opposite from a charitable remainder trust. Instead of the donor receiving income for a number of years and the charitable organization receiving the remainder, the charity gets the initial income and the donor gets the remainder—that is, what is left over at the end of the trust period goes back to the donor. This is a vehicle that is seldom used but should be used more often. It is especially attractive for people who have available cash in their younger years that they can use for charitable purposes, but want to make certain that they have the necessary funds to take care of themselves in their later years or to leave for family members.

I first used the charitable lead trust when a mother of three was killed in a car accident. She was a nurse, and her husband wanted to establish some nursing scholarships in memory of his wife. She had a life insurance policy with a face value of $25,000, but it also included a double indemnity clause, meaning the policy would pay double if the insured was accidentally killed. So, the family received $50,000. The husband used the first $25,000 for his family, and he established a 10-year charitable lead trust with the other $25,000.

The nursing school of the local community college received the income from the trust for 10 years, and the husband received the remainder at the end of the 10 years, which he allocated for his children's education. By using the charitable lead trust, he was able to accomplish both objectives: establish a scholarship fund now and have money when he needed it later. It was a definite win-win arrangement. The institution invested the money in a very good mutual fund that produced more income than was anticipated, and the remainder of the trust, which the family received when the trust terminated, had a greater financial value than had been projected. The charitable lead trust is attractive particularly to younger people, and more institutions should promote and use it.

5. The pooled income fund is another instrument used in deferred giving. Although it is also considered a trust agreement, it is very different from either of the two remainder trusts. With the pooled income fund, a donor transfers money or securities to a qualified charitable organization, designated as the remainder organization. The gift is co-mingled with the gifts of other donors to the pooled-income fund of the charitable organization. This fund, however, must be maintained separately from other assets of the organization.

Each year the total income from the fund is distributed on a pro-rata basis to the various donors or their designees. The donor's pooled income gift can also provide a life income for another person, usually a spouse or family member. Each year, for as long as they live, the respective beneficiaries receive their annual pro rata share of income generated by the fund that year. As beneficiaries die, the value of their respective shares are removed from the fund and turned over to the NFP.

This is a very easy fund to start, but there must be at least two people making contributions **on the same day** when the fund is started. The two people can be a husband and wife, as long as they write separate checks for their respective contributions. Many people fail to grasp the importance of having more than one contributor. Legally, it is absolutely necessary. A *pooled* income fund means that two or more donors are involved from day one. This requirement becomes irrelevant after the fund has been started with more than one person.

6. The charitable gift annuity is a very popular giving vehicle, especially among older people. It is an income plan and a contract, not a trust agreement. It works this way. In return for a gift of cash, securities, or other property, a charitable organization agrees to pay a fixed sum of money to one or two people for as long as they live. Part of the money paid annually to the beneficiary(s) is taxed as ordinary income and part is considered a charitable gift and is tax-free. The donor will also receive a charitable deduction in the year the gift is given. With the charitable remainder trusts and the pooled income fund, the annual income guaranteed to the beneficiary(s) is secured only by the assets of the donor's gift. That is, if the assets of the trust are exhausted, the income ceases. With the charitable gift annuity, however, the life payments are backed by the charity's entire assets, not just by the property contributed. As long as the NFP has assets, the donors will receive their payments.

The beneficiary(s) receives a fixed sum, usually a stated percentage of the gift, and it cannot be changed. These percentages, which vary from one annuity to another, are based on things like the age of the donor, the age(s) of the beneficiary(s), whether the donor gives cash or other kinds of property, when the annual payments are to begin, etc. The older the beneficiary, the higher the percentage rate will be, and the charitable deduction will also be greater. The most common way to determine the rate of return is by using the tables suggested by the American Council on Gift Annuities (formerly called the Committee on Gift Annuities), an NFP that was established in 1927 and is best known for periodically setting these percentages. Although it is not mandatory for a charity to follow the guidelines of the American Council on Gift Annuities, their rates have long been accepted by state insurance commissions (in most states the agency that oversees annuities) and the IRS. If you do not use these rates, you may have to justify to a governmental agency and the IRS that your rates are valid—that is, fair for both the donor and the NFP and that the tax considerations meet the requirements imposed by statutes and regulations.

Older people find the charitable gift annuity to be especially attractive for several reasons. They are able to donate to charity and, at the same time, generate some income for themselves. The rates are historically considerably higher than those generated by savings accounts and other safe interest-bearing investments. For example, a person 70 years old making a cash contribution in 2003 in exchange for an annuity would receive a life income at the rate of 6.7% of the contribution.[3] Of that 6.7% return, 62% would be tax-free and only 38% would be taxed as ordinary income.[4] The donor would also be eligible for a charitable deduction of 34% for income tax purposes in the year 2003. Depending on how long the annuitant lives, the charity involved will usually end up with between 40% and 50% of the original gift. One can get higher rates from a commercial annuity, but there would be no gift for a charity. You can see that these rates are very attractive. They go up and down as general interest rates change but are almost always much higher than the rate of return on other interest-bearing investments that are reputable and relatively safe. Existing annuities are not affected by rate-of-return changes; the percentage established at the time the gift is donated and the annuity agreement signed holds for the life of the annuitant(s).

In most states charitable gift annuities are closely regulated, usually by the state insurance commission. It is absolutely crucial that you check the regulations not only of the state in which your NFP is located, but also the states where people who enter into annuity agreements with your organization reside. Additionally, it is important to get several gift annuities contracted for as soon as possible after initiating a gift annuity program. The rates are based on actuarial tables and are calculated by using averages for several lives. If your organization has only one or two gift annuities, the percentages may not reflect the usual averages. The charitable gift annuity is a more difficult program to get started, but once under way, it is a very popular giving vehicle. By encouraging the use of the charitable gift annuity, your NFP will raise much money over a period of years and will make your contributors and their families very happy.

7. The deferred payment charitable gift annuity works the same way as the regular charitable gift annuity except that a person defers to a later time the date that the annuity payments will begin. Those payments can be deferred for a short period—a year or two—or for several years. The longer the payments are deferred, the higher the rate of return. People who are close to retirement and are in higher income tax brackets may want to donate the money now, when they need the charitable deduction, but defer the annuity payments to later years, when their income will probably be less and their tax brackets lower.

Deferring the payments for only three to five years can make a substantial difference in the percentage rate of return—as much as 1% to 3% more. Investing in deferred payment charitable gift annuities is an especially attractive way for people in their forties who are making good incomes to prepare for retirement and, at the same time, support a charitable organization. For example, a person who is 43 years old and makes a gift in the year 2003 in exchange for an annuity that would start making payments when he or she is 65 years old would receive a charitable deduction of 25.9% for income tax purposes in the year 2003, and the rate of return for the annuity payments, which would begin in 2024, would be 19%,[3] and 19.6% of that would be tax-free income.[5] Those are very attractive rates! A relatively new deferred gift annuity, called the tuition annuity, can provide yearly payments for a child or grandchild for four or five years for college tuition. There are several variations of the deferred payment annuity, and I am surprised that more organizations do not focus on this giving vehicle. It is a real winner with considerable flexibility for the imaginative investor.

Regardless of the size or purpose of the NFP trying to attract donors, I strongly recommend using as many different giving vehicles as possible. Smaller organizations will find it more difficult to use some of the giving vehicles than the larger institutions will, but all of the giving vehicles described can be used by almost any charitable group. Sometimes it may be more appropriate for small organizations to work with a regional office or peer group in initiating and administering some of the vehicles. It is common for small churches to work through their state or national denominational offices in establishing and sustaining their deferred giving programs. The more giving vehicles that are offered to potential contributors, the more money will be raised.

Receiving Non-Money Gifts

Step 8 of ***The System*** also calls for NFPs to be flexible in receiving gifts other than money. NFPs, including churches, educational institutions of all levels, hospitals, service clubs, labor unions, all levels of government, and political parties, to mention only a few, have long been effective in recruiting scores of volunteers to serve in all sorts of capacities. The annual value of these volunteer services runs into the hundreds of billions of dollars.[6] In addition to volunteer services, it is important to be proactive in soliciting other non-monetary gifts that have value to your group.

Charitable organizations and institutions, especially larger ones, have long been accepting gifts other than money: land, buildings, entire farms, valuable art, coin collections, office equipment and supplies, etc. They have been accepted enthusiastically because such gifts add value to the bottom line. Smaller NFPs are not as likely to solicit non-monetary gifts, but they should. By failing to do so they are missing an untapped resource that can generate much money and enthusiasm.

I have mentioned only a few of the most popular types of non-monetary gifts. But there are many more. Numerous examples follow.

Valuable items. Several years ago, when the value of gold had escalated to above $800 per ounce, the governing board of a rather small church in southern California encouraged its members to contribute gold jewelry to the building fund. The contributions to the building fund had greatly dwindled, and the board members were looking for a gimmick that might create renewed interest in the fund as well as raise $5,000. The church leaders did not anticipate the magnitude of the response nor the magnitude of the problems the response would create.

People who did not have cash to donate came forward with all sorts of gold jewelry, both expensive and inexpensive. Members also asked neighbors and friends to donate old jewelry. Surprisingly, non-members donated almost as much as members. When word got around about the success, people started donating other items, especially non-gold finery, glassware, and antique furniture. The special campaign was extended from 10 days to three months, raised almost $90,000, and ended with a celebration banquet.

Handling the non-monetary contributions was cumbersome. The church had to arrange for adequate and safe storage; the jewelry was vulnerable to professional thieves, and many of the antiques were fragile. Everything had to be taken to trustworthy gold, jewelry, and antique dealers. It was time consuming to get top-dollar for the various goods. Some items were sold immediately and others were left on consignment. The church needed many more volunteers than anticipated, and reporting to contributors the value of their gifts became a bookkeeping nightmare. Problems aside, the church was thrilled with its results, which far surpassed its most optimistic projections.

Use of buildings, classrooms, and offices. When I was president of a small college in Kentucky, the school had an immediate need for additional classrooms, especially for our expanding computer offerings. No empty buildings within a reasonable distance of the college were available for rent or purchase. I approached a local bank about the possibility of using some of its unused upstairs rooms. The bank not only agreed to let the college use the rooms rent free, it also paid for painting and carpeting the rooms, installing the additional wiring needed for the computers, and for the electricity used by the college in those rooms. The bank was located three blocks from the campus, and merchants were pleased to have the additional student traffic in the business section of town. The classrooms were not the most ideal size and shape, and the students were occasionally too noisy. Both the bank and the college experienced some inconvenience, but the arrangements were more than adequate and filled the gap until an adequate building could be acquired and refurbished.

Donated vehicles. Currently several national and local charities encourage people to contribute their used vehicles. These NFPs try to make it very convenient to do so. They will pick up (or tow away) your vehicle and complete the necessary paperwork. They accept vehicles of all types—cars, pickups, motorcycles, motor homes, large trucks, and tractors. While many cars have little value, some cars, most often those donated by older people, are in good condition. Even though most of the contributions are of limited value, the quantity of vehicles tallies up to a substantial sum.

Royalties/Commissions. I knew a middle-aged college professor who was a successful textbook writer. Although he made relatively good money, he had not saved much discretionary cash. He unconditionally transferred all of the copyrights of two of his books to his church and his university, making them the irrevocable and rightful owners of all the copyrights.

I have also known commissioned sales people who forego their commissions on sales of certain items or on all commissions over a certain amount. They have their commissions paid directly to the NFP. Such arrangements require extra paperwork and, sometimes, prove to be inconvenient. But it is money the NFP would not have otherwise received.

Insurance. Gifts of insurance have become a popular way to contribute money to one's favorite charities. Insurance gifts can be beneficial to the donor and the NFP. There are many ways a person may contribute insurance. One of the more popular ways after the insured's children are through college and have become established on their own is for the insured to exchange a whole life policy for a paid up life policy and to make the NFP the owner and beneficiary of the new policy. With this arrangement the policy holder no longer has to pay premiums, receives a tax deduction for making a charitable contribution, is able to help the charity, and does no disservice or harm to other family members. The NFP can cancel the policy and immediately receive its current cash value or keep the policy until the insured dies and receive the full death benefit. Attorneys, accountants, and insurance professionals should be consulted about the many ways of contributing life insurance policies.

Stocks. Contributing stocks has long been a popular practice. There is one cardinal rule in contributing securities. If the stocks you want to contribute have **depreciated in value** since you purchased them, you should sell the stocks and give the proceeds to the NFP. This way you will be able to use the capital loss to your advantage when preparing your income tax returns, as well as being able to take a charitable gift deduction. If the stocks you want to contribute have **appreciated in value**, you should give the stocks directly to the NFP rather than selling them first. In so doing, you will be entitled to a charitable deduction for income tax purposes equal to the current value of the stocks, and you will not have to pay any capital gains taxes on the amount of the appreciation. Again, it is important to consult professionals to make certain that the transactions are handled in the in the most advantageous ways for everyone concerned.

Be selective

The types of non-monetary gifts you receive will be determined by the needs of your NFP and your creativity. Although these items can increase your bottom line, it is important to solicit only those items that will have value for your NFP. When I was a student in divinity school, I was also serving as a student minister in a small, nearby church. I still remember how excited I was when someone offered to give the small church an upright piano that was "in very good shape." A member of the church with a pickup truck, two other members, and I went to the donor's house to get the piano. In reality, it was not in great shape, and we decided to store the piano in my garage until we could decide where to use it. This same scenario happened six more times, making a total of seven pianos and no automobile in our garage. The church finally had to pay for hauling all seven pianos to the city dump.

A similar problem can arise for schools, libraries, and churches where gifts of computers and books are concerned. Many times donors believe that their contributions have value and think they are being helpful to donate them, but in reality they have little or no value. Unfortunately, some donors may merely be looking for a charitable deduction for income tax purposes and a place to unload their unwanted items. It is important to learn when and how to say "no, thank you."

Conclusion

Step 8 of ***The System*** will enable your NFP to increase its contributions by: (1) encouraging the use of assorted giving vehicles and (2) proactively soliciting non-monetary gifts, both goods and services. Most smaller nonprofit organizations and institutions will usually have a more difficult time instituting this step because they have fewer staff members to help with the additional work involved and a smaller range of gift-giving expertise. This may be the time the services of an outside consultant are needed. It will be well worth the additional time and effort for all NFPs, regardless of size or mission statement, to find ways to make Step

8 a reality in their fund-raising efforts.

NOTES TO CHAPTER 8

1. Good places to start learning more details about various giving vehicles can be found on pp. 11-29 and 83-131 of *The Guide to Planned Giving, 2002, 8th Edition*, Paul H. Schneiter (Editor), published by The Taft Group, Farmington Hills, MI 48831-3535; Planned Giving Resources at www.pgresources.com; and American Council of Gift Annuities at www.acga-web.org.

2. At that time merchants processed a credit card charge by completing information about the purchase on a paper form that included the merchant's name and identification code, inserting the form and the customer's credit card into a small embossing machine, embossing the information from the card onto the paper form by manually pushing a roller over the card, telephoning the credit card company to get an authorization for the amount of the charge, and having the purchaser sign the form. The merchant would then mail the form or a group of completed forms to the credit card company and receive a regular paper check from the credit card company to deposit in the merchant's bank account. It did not take long for an electric roller to be developed that eliminated the necessity for manually embossing the information from the card to the form. All this just seemed too unwieldy for a worship service.

3. The financial calculations for the charitable gift annuity and the deferred payment charitable gift annuity were provided by the Office of Planned Giving, Washington University in St. Louis, MO, and are based on the rates approved by the American Council of Gift Annuities, effective Jan. 1, 2003.

4. After 15.9 years the full amount of the yearly annuity would be taxed as ordinary income.

5. After 19.9 years the full amount of the yearly annuity would be taxed as ordinary income.

6. Independent Sector, in a study based on numerous surveys, concludes that as many as 83.9 million American adults volunteer an equivalent of over 9 million full-time employees at a value of $239 billion. See *Giving and Volunteering in*

the United States, 2001, a signature series conducted and published by Independent Sector, Oct. 28, 2002.

CHAPTER 9

STEP 9: EMPHASIZE PROJECT SUPPORT.

Have you ever wondered why a car salesperson encourages customers to test-drive a car, even if they do not seem overly interested in buying one? They want customers to experience the car: the "new-car" smells, the comfort of the seats, the latest gadgets, the excitement of sitting behind the wheel, and the emotion of driving a new car. When this happens, prospective buyers are more likely to want the car. And if buyers really want a new car, they are more likely to find ways to pay for it. Salespeople do not begin with a presentation on how much the car is going to cost; they first get us interested in the concept of owning a new car. Fund-raisers need to take this page from the sales book.

Too often, the initial focus in fund-raising is on the amount of money instead of what the money will be used for. You will find that fund-raisers tend to stress the goal of how much money needs to be raised versus why the money is needed and how it will be used. This may seem natural given that the main purpose of fund-raising is to raise money. But the initial emphasis should always be on the project the money will fund—not on the money. This is important for three reasons: (1) fund-raisers are more successful in asking for contributions if they are completely convinced of the value of and need for the project; (2) people in the United States usually find a way to get what they really want; and (3) focusing on need instead of money not only takes into consideration where you are now but also sets standards for the future.

In fund-raising circles, emphasizing the project for which the money will be used versus the amount of money that is needed is called "project support." Step 9 of ***The System*** calls for emphasizing project support. If the project is properly emphasized, the money will more readily become available.

This chapter will focus on four areas: effective project reports, how project support works, types of foundations, and resources for foundations.

Effective Project Reports

To be successful in fund-raising it is necessary to have specific monetary goals. Experienced development officers always go into a campaign knowing how much money they need to raise and how it will be allocated. Throughout the campaign they make reports relative to the financial goal. They present charts and graphs depicting how much money is needed or how close they are toward reaching a specific financial figure. Under subscribing or oversubscribing the targeted figure is presented in dollar amounts or percentages of the goal. But I have rarely seen presentations illustrating what will or will not be accomplished by the amount of money being raised.

Emphasizing project support makes a big difference. It focuses people on thinking about the successful completion of a project instead of on how much money is needed. When that happens they innately direct their energies toward successfully completing the project, regardless of how much it costs. To some people, these two approaches seem similar. But there is a real difference between emphasizing project support versus raising a specific dollar figure.

How Project Support Works

Most people are not motivated by the thought of saving a certain amount of money but on getting a specific item they want. For example, a person does not think "I want $25,000"; instead, he or she concludes, "I want that new house, and it will require a down payment of $25,000." We first think of what we want or need, next determine how much money it will cost, and finally figure out how to get the money to make the purchase. Even when saving for retirement, we first think about what our needs will be and then place a price tag on them. Right or wrong, when we set our minds on getting something, we usually figure out a way to come up with the money needed.

Fund-raisers need to position their funding appeals to capitalize on our natural way of thinking when buying something. If we develop a passion for a specific charitable project, determine that it is worthwhile and needed, we will find ways to fund it. Everyone connected with the funding effort—those who are asking and those who are giving—needs to think in terms of supporting the project. When this happens, our natural instincts, passions, and emotions take over, and the funding goals are much more likely to be reached.

Project support works regardless of the size or the purpose of the financial campaign. For example, suppose a YMCA needs to purchase four houses adjacent to its property to expand its building and parking. Once purchased, there will be many sub-projects: dismantling the houses, reserving some land for an addition to the building, and keeping the remainder for paved parking. The entire project will need to be broken down into bits and pieces and a price tag put on each one. The land will cost so much a square foot; encourage people to pledge to buy a certain number of square feet. An estimated number of bulldozer hours will be needed at so much an hour; let people pledge funding for so many hours of grading. A landscaping plan, including the cost of grass seed, shrubbery, fertilizer, etc., should be posted, giving people opportunities to fund portions of it. If a building is being erected, all parts of it can be priced: the linear feet of 2 x 4's needed, the number of bricks required, so many squares of shingles for the roof, windows for outside walls, drywall for inside walls, so many gallons of paint, the rolls of carpet needed, and so on. If a scholarship program is being funded, think in terms of the cost per day of classroom time, of dormitory space, of textbooks, of a single meal. If emergency funds are needed to make up a cash-flow shortfall for the current operating budget, instead of asking for money talk about the programs that will have to be eliminated and the services that will be cut, again placing price tags on every aspect of the programs or services that are affected by the shortfall.

By using project support, very large projects are broken down into small, realistic components, making it possible for people of all economic means to participate in meaningful ways. Even children and high-school youth can participate. Several young people may band together to pledge support for a portion of a project. A single mother will find ways that she and her children will be able to help support a program. A family will be able to pledge support for the items they can afford. Some of the more affluent donors may underwrite an entire building, a room, or the furnishings for a room.

Regardless of the size or the mission of the NFP, successful fund-raisers need to provide appropriate information about a project so prospective contributors will want to support it and make it a reality. When donors get sold on the mission, they will find the money. Fund-raisers will raise more money when they emphasize project support versus goals in dollar amounts.

There are many ways to focus on project support, but each project needs to be examined separately. Each cadre of prospective donors will need to be approached differently. Fund-raisers and administrators must devise creative ways to communicate need and to ignite the passion of prospective donors toward project-specific support. Project support is about getting both the askers and the givers in the mindset of forgetting about the money and thinking in terms of the successful completion of the project. When that happens the necessary funds will follow.

Project Support via Foundations

I have chosen to address foundation grants in this chapter because they are a form of project support. When seeking financial support from a foundation, you should ask for support for a particular project; never go to a foundation to ask for money. The key to success is to identify and attract foundations that support projects similar to yours. Remember, Step 3 of ***The System***—think of yourself as a matchmaker.

A foundation is a non-governmental not-for-profit organization with its own funds and managed by its own trustees or directors. Its primary purpose is to award financial grants to NFPs for the purpose of maintaining or aiding educational, social, charitable, religious, or other activities serving the common welfare. Foundations are recognized by the IRS and are governed by laws and regulations. There are four primary types of foundations: independent, company-sponsored, community, and operating. The first three are generally thought of as grant-making foundations; operating foundations do not usually make grants.

An **Independent foundation** is a fund or endowment whose primary purpose is to make grants to other NFPs. It is designated by the IRS as a *private* foundation and is recognized as such under the law. It derives its funds primarily from a single source, usually a family or several members and friends of the family. With well-known foundations, it is not uncommon for additional contributions to be given via individual bequests and endowments. Sometimes, depending upon the source of its funding and the purpose for which the foundation exists, an independent foundation may be popularly referred to as a family or special-purpose foundation. Nearly 90% of all non-governmental grants are awarded by independent foundations.

Company-sponsored foundations are, by law, also *private*, not-for-profit funds or endowments, but they derive their funds primarily from a profit-making company or corporation. The foundation is independently constituted and controlled for the purpose of making grants to other NFPs, with or without regard for the company or corporation's business interests.

This foundation is distinct from corporate-giving programs that are administered from within the corporation and funded directly from corporate funds. Corporate-giving programs make contributions to organizations and individuals for a variety of charitable and benevolent purposes, but they are not considered grants. A majority of larger corporations have established a foundation for their major charitable-giving programs, but also maintain corporate giving programs for the purpose of making small charitable gifts to local organizations (schools, sports teams, youth groups, etc.), to local citizens or families with special financial needs, and to employees who have a family member facing a crisis that entails unusual financial outlays. Many times the corporate-giving programs will have employee representatives on the administering committees. Sometimes, the corporation will contribute funds from its foundation when the fund-raiser has requested a contribution from the corporate giving program, or vice versa. When the funds requested are not available and the executives responsible for making decisions about the company's charitable contributions really want to fund the project they may turn to the alternative source of funding.

Smaller companies and corporations tend to have either a corporate-giving program or a foundation, but usually not both. When that is the case, all of its charitable giving is channeled through the one agency, and contributions usually are localized. Most small mom-and-pop companies do not have foundations but make charitable contributions directly from company funds.

Corporations support the non-profit sector in many other ways for which they get little credit and no tax deductions. They include such things as donated services, free or low-cost use of facilities, loaned personnel, and permitting employees to volunteer on company time. It is estimated that they also spend nearly $1.5 billion annually in sponsorships.[1]

Community foundations are similar to independent foundations except that their funds are derived primarily from many donors rather than from only one or a few. A community foundation is classified as a *public* charity and is, therefore, subject to different laws and regulations than those governing a *private* foundation. The community foundation gives grants almost entirely to organizations within the local community or immediate surrounding area. The community foundation will usually have a governing board comprised of more members than most private foundations, and they will represent the broad spectrum of community interests.

Operating foundations exist primarily to fund research, social welfare, and other programs determined by its governing body. Most do not award grants to outside organizations; they fund only activities within their own organization that qualify under the charter of the foundation. The operating foundation does not normally qualify as a *grant-making* foundation, but it is recognized by the IRS and is lawfully constituted and operated as a foundation. For the practical purposes of a fund-raiser, there are only three types of grant-making foundations, and it is a waste of your time and energy to seek a grant from most operating foundations.

The Special Category of Government Grants

There is one other category of grants not yet addressed—government grants. Departments, agencies, and institutes associated with the United States Government award millions of dollars in grants to universities, hospitals, and other NFPs each year. For example, the U. S. Department of Education provides resources for research on school quality in the United States and for international exchange programs; the National Institute on Health provides resources for research on HIV/AIDS and many other diseases; the U. S. Institute of Peace provides resources for research on peace-related topics (e.g., disarmament, democratization, etc.) and for educational programs related to peace and security. These and many other government agencies typically require long and detailed applications that favor well-known specialists in whatever field is being targeted by the government grant.

Such grants are very competitive and are hardly ever prepared by regular development personnel or professional fund-raisers. Writing successful grants for government agencies is a specialty and something of an "art form," and relatively few people know how to write successful proposals for government grants. Such grants are an important source of money for some institutions and organizations in the country. But because of their high level of specialization, they are not the focus of this book and are not discussed.

A Top Resource For Fund-Raisers—The Foundation Center

The Foundation Center, headquartered in New York City, is the most authoritative source of information available about foundations. It was established and funded by foundations in 1960 as a national service organization to provide a single authoritative source of information about foundations and corporate giving in the United States. Still funded by foundations, its publications and on-line data are the primary sources of information used by grant seekers. Much of the statistical information in this chapter can be found in various publications of The Foundation Center and on its website.[2]

The Center offers many annual directories, CD-ROMs, on-line searchable databases, educational courses, and workshops. There is a charge for most of these publications and services. Regional and state publications that have been produced jointly by The Foundation Center or in cooperation with the Center are valuable sources of information that are many times overlooked. The Center also makes available to the public **free of charge** a nationwide network of **Center Libraries and Cooperating Collections** located in more than 200 cities. Every state has at least one; larger states have up to the mid twenties. Basic directories and other important data, including CD-ROMs, are available through each of these

Center Libraries; some have more complete collections than others. If your local branch of the Center Libraries and Cooperating Collection does not have an article or a book, there is an interlibrary loan program. A complete list of all the Center Libraries and Cooperating Collections is available from The Foundation Center. The Center may be contacted by mail (The Foundation Center, 79 Fifth Avenue, New York, NY 10003-30760), by telephone (1-800-424-9836), or online (www.fdncenter.org).

The Foundation Center maintains the **Online Library** where you may submit questions about foundations and corporate giving. Usually within 24 to 36 hours you will receive answers to your questions or suggestions for where you are most likely to find the answers. Questions may be submitted to the Librarian of the Foundation Center Online Library (www.library@fdncenter.org).

Although The Foundation Center annually publishes several sources of information, most grant seekers will initially want to concentrate on two of them: *The Foundation Directory* and *The Foundation Directory, Part 2*. These two directories contain information on the top 20,000 foundations based on total dollar amount of grants awarded during the current year. The most current edition of both should be available at all Center Libraries and Cooperating Collections. Both directories have a variety of invaluable indexes covering a wide range of categories that grant seekers should find helpful.

The Foundation Directory publishes extensive information about our country's 10,000 largest foundations in terms of total dollar amount of all grants awarded for that year. These 10,000 foundations award more than 90% of all dollars awarded by grant-making foundations in the United States. The information is gathered from several public sources, including government records, tax returns, and foundation reports. There are 34 possible data elements for each foundation's entry. However, at least during one's **initial** stages of research about any foundation, the data of greatest interest would be: name, address, and telephone number of the foundation; person in the foundation to contact for information; types of support and fields of interest for which grants are made; grant restrictions, such as geographic locations or types of organizations; how to apply to the foundation for a grant; dates grants are issued; deadlines for receiving grant applications; history of the foundation's most recent grants; and names and titles of officers, principal administrators, and trustees/directors.

The Foundation Directory, Part 2, similar to the first, contains information for what is usually referred to as the "second tier" of grant-making foundations—that is, the nation's next 10,000 largest foundations in terms of the total dollar amount of their grants. It uses the same format as *The Foundation Directory*.

Each year, about six months after the publication of these two directories, the *Supplement* is published. It updates any of the entries that have had substantial changes since they were published. Weekly updates can be found on The Foundation Center's web site for a one-time user fee or for an on-going subscription fee.

If your NFP is actively engaged in seeking numerous grants from several foundations, I recommend that you subscribe to The Foundation Center's on-line services. But if you are seeking only an occasional grant, it will be more cost effective to pay only for those services that are needed from time to time. All of the information needed for grant seekers is available in the print versions of the Foundation Center's various directories, most of which can be found in any of the Center Libraries and Cooperating Collections. If you are looking for a specific periodical article or directory other than *The Foundation Directory, The Foundation Directory, Part 2,* and the *Supplement*, telephone ahead to make certain they have a copy.

As you get further along in your search for foundation grants, there are two other publications that you will probably want to look at: the *National Directory of Corporate Giving: A Guide to Corporate Giving Programs and Corporate Foundations* and the *Guide to U. S. Foundations, their Trustees, Officers, and Donors*. Both are published annually by The Foundation Center, and both are found in most of the Center Libraries and Cooperating Collections. Their titles are indicative of their contents.

Websites are a fast-growing way for foundations to report to the public and to make their giving guidelines and application requirements known to grant seekers. Fewer than 20% of all foundations provide any printed materials; most smaller foundations do not provide printed reports or brochures.[3] A good source of information about the use of the internet in contacting foundations is *The Fund Raiser's Guide to the Internet* (disk included), by Michael Johnson, the NSFRE/Wiley Fund Development Series, published by John Wiley & Sons, Inc., NY, 1999.

Tapping into the Smaller Foundations

In addition to the 20,000 foundations listed in the two main directories, there are more than 50,000 other active grant-making foundations in the United States (and close to 20,000 more very small foundations that are currently inactive).[4] Many of these are very small and give only a few hundred dollars in grants each year, while others are somewhat larger and may give $3,000 to $5,000 each year. Most of these smaller foundations are very localized in the NFPs they support. It is not always easy to find information about them, but these smaller foundations are a significant source of financial support that most fund-raisers ignore or overlook. Believe me, this is a big mistake!

For years I paid little attention to the small, localized foundations that were not listed in one of The Foundation Center's major directories. I assumed that there was not much money to be had from these sources, many of which were "mom-and-pop" foundations with very limited financial resources. I then stumbled across a relatively new, very small family foundation listed in a state directory housed as part of the Center Libraries and Cooperating Collections in Louisville, Kentucky. I telephoned the contact person, and she was so excited as I was the first person to contact her about a grant since the foundation was established three years prior. She invited me to visit her and her husband, which I did two days later. I left their home with a $3,000 check, the total amount that the foundation had available to contribute at that time, to be used by the institution as I designated. It was the easiest foundation grant I ever received—one telephone call, no written proposal, one hour on the road each way, and two hours at the foundation office (which included lunch around the kitchen table). Additionally, for the next two years our institution received all of the grants awarded by this small foundation. Since that event, I have spent a lot of time researching and contacting small, seldom-listed and little-known foundations, and I have been turned down only once.

If your requests are reasonable, have emotional appeal, and are in line with the giving guidelines of the foundation, there is much money to be received from these very small foundations. Of course, it takes many more grants from these smaller foundations to equal the dollars of a single large grant. But in most cases, the smaller grants take much less time and effort to obtain, and there is less competition for them. Furthermore, you are more likely to extend your long-term financial security by broadening your giving base to include as many different contributors as possible; it becomes less disruptive when, for whatever reason, you lose the support of one or several of your donors. I always recommend that fund-raisers rely more on small gifts from numerous contributors than large gifts from only a few. This strategy also applies to foundations.

Since nearly all of these small foundations do not publish an annual report, it may take some effort to "dig out" the needed information. I believe that the best place to start learning about these smaller foundations is at one of the Center Libraries and Cooperating Collections. The librarians at most of these Center Libraries are very knowledgeable and will be of considerable assistance to you in learning about some of the smaller, less-known foundations in your locality. If you do not receive the assistance you need at your local Center Libraries and Cooperating Collections, you should contact The Foundation Center in New York City.

In most metropolitan areas, in addition to the Center Libraries and Cooperation Collections, there are one or more **local and state associations or agencies** that exist for the purpose of assisting NFP fund-raisers and fund-givers. They, too, are a likely source of information about the smaller foundations. (Do not confuse these agencies with the many fund-raising counselors and organizations that are primarily funded by the for-profit sector and are listed in the yellow pages of telephone directories.) Another possible source of information is a directory of foundations located in your state or area. If such a directory exists, it will probably include both the large and small foundations. I do not know of any directory that lists only the smaller foundations. Although there is no foundation directory for many states, there are several regional directories that have information about a several-state area.

Tax form 990-PF, the tax return that all private foundations are required to file with the IRS, is the only source I know of that includes all grants made by private foundations. Copies of the 990-PF's are public information, and they may be the only reliable source of information about the very small foundations in your state. GrantSmart.org, a searchable database for tax-related information for all active grant-making private foundations, is one source for all 990-PF's filed (www.grantsmart.org).

You will find that most of the smaller foundations are part of an unofficial network. When you locate two or three, they will usually help get you in touch with other ones. Most of the people connected with these smaller foundations are eager to work with development professionals and will respond with a great deal of appreciation and loyalty.

Basics To Remember When Working With Foundations

Through the years I have had very few foundation proposals rejected. I attribute my success in securing foundation grants to my following the basic guidelines outlined below.

- Foundations exist for the purpose of giving away money. They are required by law to give away a certain percentage of their assets each year. Do not be afraid to contact foundations.

- Before contacting a foundation, make every effort to verify that your needs and the foundation's giving guidelines are a match. Remember Step 3 of The System—think of yourself as a matchmaker. Do not waste your time or the foundation's time on a proposal that, regardless of how worthy, is outside the scope of the foundation's current giving guidelines.

- Whenever possible, speak with someone on the administrative staff of a foundation about your idea in general terms prior to submitting a proposal. During such a conversation you will usually be either encouraged or discouraged from submitting your actual proposal.

- Give yourself plenty of time to prepare the proposal. Good proposals are not developed overnight.

- Follow the foundation's procedures for submitting proposals, even if they do not make sense to you. Be especially careful to meet all deadlines. If you are unable to follow directions and meet deadlines, foundations will doubt your ability to administer a grant properly. Most foundations have specified periods and dates for proposals to be acted upon by their governing boards. Board meetings are usually scheduled annually, semi-annually, and quarterly. Larger foundations tend to meet once a year to award grants, while smaller, less structured foundations usually meet at least annually but may convene at other times of the year if proposals are presented for their consideration. Many excellent proposals receive no consideration at all because they miss the submission deadlines.

- Always be considerate of the demands that face foundation personnel on a daily basis and try to make their jobs as easy as possible. Most foundations are understaffed. Remember that you are among thousands of grant seekers. It has been my experience that if you set yourself apart by being unusually considerate of foundation personnel, they will frequently reciprocate, which is incredibly beneficial. On several occasions, foundation administrators have actually assisted me in crafting my proposal so that it would be more likely to gain board approval. I think in some instances they helped me not only because they thought my proposal was worthy but also because they thought I would be pleasant to work with in administering the grant.

- Keep grant proposals short and to the point. This may come as a surprise to some people, but I strongly recommend that, unless directed to do otherwise by the respective foundation, all foundation proposals should not exceed three pages in length and be accompanied by a cover letter of only one page. Many of my funded proposals were only two pages in length, and some were only one page. The purpose of the cover letter is to get the foundation's attention. The purpose of the proposal is to summarize in very distinct terms the needs you are addressing and how being awarded a grant will meet those needs. Keep in mind that foundations receive thousands of proposals and they have limited staff available to read them. If the foundation is interested in your proposal, they will ask you for additional information.

- Getting a proposal through the approval process can be an extended "work in progress" requiring numerous revisions and, in some instances, compromise. I recommend that you do not submit a proposal until you are convinced that it will be seriously considered and has at least a 75% chance of getting approved.

- When seeking a grant from a specific foundation, distribute the names of their trustees and administrative staff to your organization's trustees and staff. If anyone from your NFP knows any of the foundation's people, I strongly suggest that discreet inquiries be made on your behalf because you have a better chance of getting a hearing for your proposal. If your colleagues are hesitant to go out on a limb for you, they need to be replaced because they fail to meet Step 2—believe in the cause.

- Unless the foundation has specific guidelines to the contrary, I strongly recommend that proposals call for receiving funding in diminishing amounts over a three-year period. Foundations are very careful about selecting the NFPs they award grants to; they want to make certain the money will be used appropriately. Once they identify a worthy grantee, they usually are pleased to make repeat contributions. It has been my experience that you will receive more money by spreading a request over a three-year period rather than asking for one lump sum. When submitting a three-year proposal, one can reasonably ask that the second year's award be about one-half the amount of the first year's grant, and the third year's about one-third the original amount. Suppose you are asking for a total of $75,000. I would recommend requesting $40,000 for the first year; $20,000 for the second; and $15,000 for the third. To ensure that you receive all three awards, it is important for you to provide regular reports to the foundation. Reporting frequently on your current proposal will also greatly improve your prospects of being awarded future grants.

Conclusion

Step 9 of ***The System*** is to emphasize project support. When the primary focus is on the project being funded, donors will respond by contributing the needed funds. Although a major portion of this chapter has been devoted to foundations, please remember what was pointed out in the *Introduction*—approximately 85% of all charitable contributions from non-governmental sources comes from individuals, either through regular gifts or bequests, and seasoned fund-raising professionals will devote their primary efforts to contributions from individuals.[5] Whether with individuals or more formal entities, these gifts do not just happen. One primary key to success in fund-raising is emphasizing project support.

NOTES TO CHAPTER 9

1. *Giving USA, 2002,* pp. 96-97.

2. I have gleaned much of the information in this chapter from years of experience, and it would be difficult for me to document the specific sources. For accuracy, I have checked many of the details against the informational sources referred to in the next several paragraphs of this chapter. The primary ones come from The Foundation Center, but Internet access has brought many less well-known sources to the fore.

3. *The Chronicle of Philanthropy*, "Few Foundations Publish Reports, Study Finds," Dec. 12, 2002, p. 10.

4. As of January 17, 2003, The Foundation Center, through its Online Foundation Directory, put the number of foundations in existence in the United States at 72,848.

5. See page 8 of the Introduction and note 6 at the end of the Introduction.

CHAPTER 10

STEP 10: ALWAYS ASK FROM A POSITION OF STRENGTH.

People strive to invest their money and time in winning causes. They want to make certain that they are not putting their money into a dying endeavor. With this in mind, it is important for donors to see your NFP as a good investment, a worthy entity that has the strength and vision to survive and flourish well into the future.

Step 10 of ***The System***, "Always ask from a position of strength," may appear to be a simple concept, yet it is complex because people define strength differently. And the term takes on additional meaning when applied to NFPs and fund-raising. The definition will vary by NFPs, mission statements, organizational structures, leadership teams, and donor bases. However it is defined, suffice it to say that NFPs that are strong and ask from a position of strength are likely to raise significantly more money.

This chapter will focus on two issues: how to ask from a position of strength and how to incorporate the five W's of fund-raising. But first, let us define what is meant by strength as used in Step 10.

What Does "Asking from a Position of Strength" Really Mean?

Strength has many meanings. To grasp its far-reaching significance, I turned to *Roget's International Thesaurus* (fourth edition) where I found numerous words and phrases that are relevant to understanding the concept of strength as applied to Step 10. They include the following: durability, hardiness, stability, power, tenacity, vigor, moral fiber, vitality, strength of purpose, sturdiness, potency, effectiveness, masterfulness, drive, and force.

The System presupposes that any NFP seeking contributions embodies many of these qualities. Only NFPs that currently embody qualities of strength and are in a position to remain strong into the future, or those that currently are having difficulties but have a viable plan to get strong, should seek contributions and expect donors to respond. Unfortunately, there are some NFPs that do not meet these qualifications.

Before you assume that I have narrowed the acceptable and legitimate fund-raising causes to an elite or favored few, let me emphasize that Step 10 is applicable to all NFPs, regardless of size or mission. Even the small, little-known NFP can ask from a position of strength. Strength as used in Step 10 is not about size, but about character and procedures.

What to Do and What to Avoid

It is very important that your NFP be recognized by donors for its strength. It does not matter whether your NFP is large with many employees or small with only one or two people and an extremely limited budget. Although many things demonstrate strength, there are five key concepts that will best manifest your strength and help with your fund-raising efforts. They are:

- Show the strength and vitality of your NFP,
- Show the immediate benefits of a donation,
- Show your long-term plan for success,
- Reinforce the ethics and qualifications of your leaders and staff, and
- Personalize letters and appeals when possible.

The sections that follow elaborate on these.

First, show the strength and vitality of your organization. You want donors to know your NFP has a strong, worthwhile mission that impacts others and the community in positive ways. You also want donors to know that you have the vision and leadership to survive into the future.

I am amazed when NFPs mail requests to their potential contributors at the end of the year requesting money for emergency relief, declaring that this has been a devastating year financially, that past-due bills are piling up on their desks, that their very existence is being threatened, and that they must receive an influx of very generous contributions before the end of the year to overcome these many obstacles and survive into the next year. Does that sound like asking from a position of strength? Letters like these do not depict an organization that demonstrates durability, hardiness, stability, power, vitality, strength of purpose, sturdiness, and force. Donors do not like to waste their money on "sinking ships."

Many strong NFPs occasionally have year-end shortages. If your NFP is experiencing difficult circumstances and a financial shortfall, you need to give a plausible explanation for how these came about and a creditable strategy for overcoming them. I have seen many very effective letters calling for emergency help, but the successful ones always include a plan for solving the problems and getting out of trouble. Requesting emergency contributions year in and year out will erode your NFP's credibility and eventually result in long-term financial instability and possible extinction.

Year-end appeals are very common and can be quite successful. The end of the calendar year embodies a holiday season when most people feel especially generous and most knowledgeable donors calculate, for tax purposes, how much to contribute to charity and the best ways to do it. It is an accepted practice for NFPs to mail appeal letters at various times of the year, including holiday seasons or times of special interest to the charitable entity. But always be certain that you are asking from a position of strength.

Second, show people their money will go to immediate use. Let people know how their donations will immediately benefit your NFP and its outreach base. Americans as a whole have very high expectations and are accustomed to seeing immediate results. Your donors need to know that their contributions will make a difference.

Third, show your long-term plan for success. This can be done in both very simple and very complex ways. Some donors will want to know the details of your long-term fund-raising plan and even your five-year operational strategy. Others are satisfied just to know that a long-range plan exists and that you "look forward to serving others for years to come." The main idea is that people want to know they are making a wise investment and not giving money to a struggling group that will be forced to close its doors in two or three months.

Fourth, reinforce the ethics and qualifications of your leaders and staff. We have seen the unethical and illegal actions of corporate leaders ruin well-established companies and result in severe repercussions for innocent employees and stockholders. A few well-known and trusted NFPs have also come into the limelight. Regardless of the size or purpose of your NFP, it is crucial that your donor base trust your leadership team—paid staff, volunteers, consultants, and board members. Professional ethics is addressed in detail in Chapter 12.

Fifth, personalize appeals where possible. The more you personalize letters and appeals, the more your contributions will increase.

Far too frequently, I see form letters without an inside address, and the salutation or greeting used in the letter is something like "Dear Friend," "Dear Supporter," "Dear Contributor," "Dear Prayer Partner," or "Dear Member." The signature at the end of these letters is also the same on each letter—a printed copy of the original signature. Although form letters definitely raise money, you will consistently raise considerably more money by personalizing aspects of your letters.

In 1958, I worked as a student intern for two weeks at the Billy Graham New York Crusade. Obviously, there were no computers at the time. At the headquarters, there was a room containing a bank of electric typewriters in long lines on several tables. Each typewriter could be used manually or an electronic tape could be inserted that typed pre-programmed letters. There were several administrative assistants, and each one operated five typewriters at a time. The assistants would insert a sheet of Crusade letterhead into the typewriter, type a name, address, and personal salutation, and push a key that would start the tape. As that letter was being typed, they moved to the next typewriter and repeated the same procedure. Once the fifth typewriter was operating, the assistants would go back to the first typewriter and start the process again. Each letter was either personally signed or a signature machine was used (that is, the signature was never just a printed copy of the original).

I concluded then and there that if a huge organization sending hundreds of thousands of letters could personalize its letters, I could find a way to do the same regardless of the size or budget of the church or other NFP I might serve.

One such church had a mailing list of 3,200 people, and we mailed a personalized appeal letter to each member three times a year. I personally signed every letter, and on the great majority I wrote a PS that related to some real-life incident that the recipient had experienced that I knew about or that I had shared with them. I followed the same practice in later years as a college president. Sure, it took a lot of extra time! But I still remember a consultant we had on campus dealing with an accreditation matter saying to me, "You are the best fund-raiser I have ever known. How do you do it?"

I was unusually successful because I always took into consideration the advantages of asking from a position of strength, regardless of how much extra time, energy, or effort it took. With today's technology, it is easy to do. At a minimum, you want to personalize the name and address. Adding personalized comments, including paragraphs on special aspects of your NFP (for example, those who contributed to a special program at your NFP) will increase your contributions. The more you personalize your solicitation letters and demonstrate a caring spirit, the more money will be contributed. There is no question about it because you will be asking from a position of strength.

The Five W's of Asking From Strength

Another key ingredient of asking from a position of strength is the coordination of what I refer to as the "Five W's of Fund-raising." They are:

1. **W**ho should ask?
2. **W**ho should be asked?
3. **W**hen should they be asked?
4. **W**here should they be asked?
5. **W**here should the money be used?

Paying attention to the five W's boils down to this: if the right person asks the right person at the right time and in the right place for the right project you will definitely maximize the likelihood of increasing the total number of charitable gifts received and the total dollar amounts of those contributions. Identifying those persons, times, places, and projects prior to asking is essential to any successful financial campaign. Let us explore the five W's more closely.

Who should ask? Different circumstances dictate the use of different people in asking for charitable contributions. With every fund-raising event or campaign, much consideration must be given to identifying who should do the asking. In order to identify the best person or persons, it is essential to do your homework before the asking phase. This ensures asking from a position of strength.

The general rule is that the highest-ranking person with day-to-day operational responsibilities should ask for the contribution, whether in person or by letter. People want the opportunity to meet and see who is in charge of where their money is being contributed. Being personally contacted (via mail, telephone, or face-to-face) by the senior minister of a church, the president of a college, the executive director of an organization or agency, or the chairman of the board is usually an impressive and productive way of asking for a contribution. Given the many cases of corporate fraud and abuse revealed since 2002, it may well be more important than ever that contact be made by the person in charge.

In most cases, the development officer is the best person to do the homework and preliminary work that leads to asking for a contribution. It takes a special kind of person to be a good development officer. He or she must be very unselfish and primarily focused on the end result of raising the total number of dollars needed rather than on being the person who will do the asking or on getting the credit for bringing home the check. In some cases a special rapport will exist between the development officer and the prospective donor that warrants the development officer being the one who does the asking; more often than not, someone else ends up being selected to do the asking.

There are circumstances, however, where someone other than the person in charge is better suited to ask for a contribution, and there are many reasons for this. It is quite common, especially with the annual fund campaign or a special purpose campaign, to have members or friends (not paid professionals) associated with the charitable organization asking for the majority of the contributions. We see this in churches where members serving on committees do the asking, with colleges where students and alumni help with initial contacts and follow-up telephone calls for the annual fund drive, and with almost any kind of NFPs capital campaign where volunteers having various connections with the organization are involved in asking.

If "bad blood" exists between the top person and the prospective donor, someone else should definitely do the asking. Or, if the person in charge is relatively young and does not come from a strong financial background, it may be advisable to find someone older and with more financial experience to do the asking, especially where older people are concerned; seniors tend to trust more seasoned people in advising them about their financial matters. Or it may be that someone else in the administration or on the board has a special relationship (personal or business) that would make him or her a better person to do the asking. Especially in cases involving larger contributions, it may be advisable for a respected leader in the community or a retired banker or former business associate to do the asking or to accompany the person doing the asking.

It is important to do your homework to determine who is the best person to ask for a contribution. In many NFPs, especially smaller ones, it is the CEO's (president or executive director) responsibility to serve also as the chief fund-raiser. This is frequently a mistake because, as most of you know, being a fund-raiser involves so much more than doing the asking. The average CEO does not have the time to do all of the homework and teambuilding that is necessary for successful fund-raising. Unless the agency is very small and quite limited in its scope of activities, the CEO will be stretched too thin to be both an accomplished CEO and successful fund-raiser. It is my firm conviction that every NFP needs both a professional development officer or fundraiser and a CEO. The results will be much more rewarding.

This does not mean that the person responsible for fund-raising must be a full-timer. It is common to use consultants and part-time employees.

When using part-time employees, it is essential that they be fund-raising professionals. Some NFPs make the mistake of employing someone whose primary fund-raising experience has been raising money for NFPs by selling things—cookies, candies, T-shirts, or what-have-you—but who have no training as a professional fund-raiser for the not-for-profit sector. Their focus and training, instead, has been making money for the vendor. They lack the understanding of what fund-raising for NFPs is all about.

Nor is it acceptable to select a well-meaning, well-liked and enthusiastic person who has great affection for the organization and is willing to serve at a salary well below the going rate for such a position, or even as a volunteer, but who lacks training and experience as a professional for non-profit fund-raising.

No rational person would approve using well-meaning but untrained people in the practice of law, medicine, or any other field requiring specialized training. Similarly, we need to adhere to that same standard when selecting fund-raisers. Fund-raising is a very technical and complicated profession, and it takes someone who has been thoroughly trained in that profession to do the job.

Teamwork between the president, development officer, board, volunteers, consultants, and other staff members is essential. Beware of the person (at any level) who insists on being the only one who asks for contributions and is not willing to share the limelight. It will result in doomed or less effective results.

It is important to do your homework to determine who is the best person to do the asking.

Who should be asked? Most often, it is appropriate to go directly to the person from whom you are seeking a contribution and ask him or her directly. But there are also instances when another person or combination of people needs to be involved, consulted, or actually present when asking donors for money. For example, the available funds may be part of a family estate that several people control. Or a potential contributor may rely on a financial advisor to make recommendations concerning major donations. A wife or husband may not make any contributions without talking with each other or their adult children. An inheritance may be held in trust for a minor child or the care and maintenance of a mentally impaired adult offspring, and the appropriate person to contact is the trustee. It may be that an adult offspring handles all of the financial affairs for his or her aged mother or father or both. Again, doing one's homework will help clarify who should be asked.

Teamwork also comes to the fore in deciding who should be asked. It is sometimes important for an entire family to be involved so that some members do not feel that you are working behind their backs and cutting them out of money that would be theirs in the future. The family attorney, accountant, or financial advisor also may need to be involved.

Fund-raisers may be reluctant to involve others because they are afraid that someone else's involvement may "jinx the deal." Fund-raisers may be especially anxious to keep lawyers from participating because lawyers have the reputation for being "nit-pickers" who are overly protective of their clients and always prolong, and frequently insist on altering the transaction. In reality, many (although certainly not all) lawyers, accountants, and financial advisors do not understand the intricacies of the fund-raising vehicles available to their clients or all of the tax advantages of using them. Nevertheless, if the transaction is sound and defensible, involving other people initially may well eliminate the necessity for dealing with them later in a much more hostile atmosphere. That is all part of asking from a position of strength.

When should they be asked? Timing is one of the most crucial elements of effectively asking for a charitable contribution. Asking at the right time enhances the likelihood of receiving a gift, and asking at the wrong time can be a deathblow.

When I worked as the development officer for a community college, state law prohibited using tax dollars to fund athletic programs in community colleges. Because the college fielded several athletic teams, it was the development department's responsibility to raise the necessary funds from the public sector to pay for the athletic programs. Tuition was relatively inexpensive for local students, thanks to state, county, and city subsidies and tax dollars. This was not the case, however, for about 20 out-of-state athletes, most of whom played on the baseball and basketball teams; students from another state paid considerably higher tuition. Like most community colleges, the majority of students lived at home and commuted to the college on a daily basis. But since the college did not have a dining room, snack bar, or residence hall, a substantial amount of money had to be raised to underwrite the daily living expenses and other costs for the out-of-state athletes.

It was relatively easy to solicit funds for scholarships for out-of-state tuition, coaching salaries, uniforms and equipment, vans, acceptable housing, and travel expenses. Our stumbling block was providing adequate meals on a consistent basis. Remembering the concept of project support (Step 9), we went to the local restaurants to ask them to take turns feeding our athletes. The first person to offer his restaurant was a graduate of the college. He made a big commitment to provide the evening meal (which was the most expensive) for all the out-of-state players. He was enthusiastic about the college's program and was instrumental in getting other restaurants and fast food chains to participate. The response was very positive, and we found enough restaurants to provide the other meals.

The arrangements were completed one day before a scheduled faculty meeting, where I routinely gave regular updates on our fund-raising efforts. I generally reported on efforts that benefited the faculty. (I felt that most faculty members looked at the development office as a necessary evil to be endured, although some did appreciate that my Ph.D. degree contributed to the academic credentials of the faculty and staff.) But on that day, I proudly did some legitimate boasting; I discussed our success in underwriting the entire athletic budget and especially how generous the local restaurant owners were in providing meals for our out-of-state athletes.

The faculty meeting occurred on a Thursday, and on the following Monday I stopped in for lunch at the restaurant owned by the "always-friendly" graduate who was donating the evening meals for the athletes. On this day, however, he was not friendly; in fact, he was really irate with me. To make a long story short, the chairman of the performing arts department had visited him earlier that day. The chairman said that I had told the faculty about the generosity of the restaurant owner in providing meals for athletes, so he stopped by to solicit financial support for the well-known (but expensive) performing arts series. The restaurant owner assumed that I had sent the chairman, felt he was being taken for granted, thought he had been betrayed, was terribly hurt, and decided he would no longer support the athletic teams.

Fortunately, I was able to set the record straight quickly and salvage the situation. But I shuddered at what would have happened had I not by chance decided to eat lunch at his restaurant on that particular day.

I learned an important lesson from that incident. At the next faculty meeting we discussed the team concept and how everyone needed to work together to achieve our fund-raising goals. It is important for a college, or any NFP, to coordinate all of its fund-raising efforts by being proactive in developing a broad-based team approach. The concept of a team is used intentionally because each team has a coach, a playbook, and a game plan. If individual players take things into their own hands, ignoring the playbook and the game plan, the end result is likely to be defeat. Every fund-raising effort needs one person calling the plays from a pre-determined playbook that all the players understand and follow.

The story of the restaurant owner demonstrates how successful a fund-raising effort can be when the prospective contributor is asked for a contribution at the right time and how detrimental it can be if the donor is asked at the wrong time. We were successful in initially securing the support of the key restaurant owner because we did our homework, devised a game plan that included a time line, and went about executing the pre-determined strategy. The action of the performing arts chair was a disaster for several reasons: (1) the restaurant owner had just made a major commitment the week before; (2) based on the homework done by the development office we believed that his commitment was at the top end of the maximum amount he could afford to contribute at that time; (3) he had not been properly thanked before asking for another contribution as discussed in Chapter 11; (4) the performing arts chair had not been trained in how to ask for a charitable contribution; (5) the chair's action in going out on his own to solicit contributions was not factored into the current fund-raising plans of the development office (the official fund-raising organ of the college); and (6) the president of the college had not authorized anyone going to the private sector on behalf of the college for non-approved projects. At another time and under different circumstances, it might have been very appropriate for the chair to solicit funds from the restaurant owner as well as from many other people in the town. But not at the time he did it.

Fund-raisers should guard against imposing their own time schedules on prospective donors. This is true even if your NFP is in need of immediate funds. It is best to defer to the most convenient and appropriate time for the well-being and peace of mind of the prospective donor. It has always been my experience that if you hurry the time line of the prospective donor, you will diminish your chances of success.

Allowing enough time to ask a prospective donor and not feel hurried is also important. It often takes longer than anticipated to make a presentation and answer all of the questions. Frequently, time has to be spent with "small talk" and possibly eating a meal. I know of one case when the prospective contributor decided not to make a commitment simply because the person making the presentation kept glancing at his watch; the prospective donor felt that he had been taken for granted and was not being given the attention he deserved. (The president of the institution, who was making the presentation, had scheduled presentations at the homes of two prospective contributors on the same evening, one at 7:00 p.m. and the other only two hours later; he obviously had not allocated enough time for the first presentation.) The contribution was recouped two days later when the development officer went back to the prospective donor and spent an entire afternoon with him. It is crucial that enough time be allocated so that an orderly and thorough presentation can be made and questions can be asked and answered.

Where should they be asked? Again, your homework and research will help answer this question. It varies with different donors and circumstances. It is very important to find a place where the potential donor feels comfortable and where the person asking can make a good presentation.

When possible, I like to have prospective donors come to a place where they can actually see the NFP in action. This may mean visiting a campground, a day care center, a college campus, a counseling center, a schoolroom, an athletic field, etc. Or it may mean meeting in the office of the NFP, the senior minister, executive director, or president. It is not unusual for the asking to take place at the donor's home or office, during a meal at a restaurant, or at a golf club. Sometimes it will be done at a mass meeting where an entire audience will be asked to contribute or make a pledge. As long as the prospective donor and solicitor feel comfortable, it does not matter where the meeting takes place. Doing your homework will help you find the right place.

Where should the money be used? Finally, asking from a position of strength is respecting the prospective donor's right to decide what kind of contribution to make and how it should be used. A common failure made by development officers, especially less experienced ones, is to decide unilaterally what assets should be donated by the prospective donor, the type of vehicle that should be utilized in making the contribution, and the purpose for which the contribution is to be used.

It is easy for this to happen. For example, you may be conducting a campaign for scholarship funds, and the donor wants the contribution to be earmarked for new computers or equipment for the chemistry laboratory. You may be concentrating on immediate gifts and the donor wants, instead, to enter into a deferred-giving arrangement. You may be trying to get the initial contributions necessary to start a pooled-income fund and the donor wants to purchase a charitable-gift annuity. You may be seeking a cash contribution with no strings attached, but the donor contributes shares of stock that consistently have increased in value with the recommendation that the board adds them to the endowment fund. Many people try to talk the prospective donor into doing what the development officer or institution wants rather than listening to what the donor wants. Worst of all is when development officers stress that making the contribution as they propose will be more beneficial for the donor when that is not necessarily the case.

It is appropriate for the development officer to suggest what giving vehicle should be used and the reasoning behind such a suggestion. It is also appropriate to suggest what the current needs of the organization or institution are and to suggest contributing for one or more of those purposes. But in the end, the donor's decisions should be respected and his or her best interests protected. That kind of integrity is characteristic of what it means to ask from a position of strength.

Coordinating and executing the five W's of fund-raising is essential to asking from a position of strength. Make certain that you devise a plan to assure that the right person asks the right person at the right time and in the right place. Your research will enhance your position of strength.

The Five W's at Work

At one of the churches I served, we started a day care center. The director believed that it was important for the children to be outside as much as possible. This included daily walks in the neighborhood accompanied by one of the teachers or, on occasion, by the director. They tended to take the same route each day, passing by a large house with a bay window in front where an elderly woman could be seen sitting each day as they walked by. She would wave at the children each day, and they would wave back. One day, a housekeeper came out and invited the children in for cookies, as it was the old woman's birthday. After that the children were frequently invited in to see her.

When I learned about this I suspected that she was an ideal candidate for making a contribution to start an endowment fund for the day care center. My homework validated my suspicions; she lived in a neighborhood and house that indicated she could possibly afford a contribution, she had never been married, had no close relatives, and, in fact, would appreciate having an opportunity to use some of her money on behalf of the children.

I felt without question that the director should be the one asking for the contribution. She believed so wholeheartedly in the cause, knew better than anyone else the needs, and was truly sincere when talking about the center. But she had never before solicited a gift and was petrified by the thought of asking the old woman. Eventually, however, I prevailed.

She stopped by to talk with the prospective donor, spent two hours with her, and left with a check for $26,000. This is a perfect example of the five W's in action. The right person asked the right person at the right time at the right place for the right project. Had any one of these five components not been present, the day care center would not have received the donation.

A Quick Note On Foundations

Most of this chapter deals with individuals and families. When approaching foundations the specifics of the five W's are usually outlined in the foundation guidelines and will be addressed in the proposal presented to the foundation. As mentioned in Chapter 9, when preparing a grant request for a foundation it is essential to meet deadlines, be a matchmaker, and follow foundation procedures. These are all ingredients in submitting a grant proposal from a position of strength.

Conclusion

Step 10 of ***The System*** is not so much about introducing a new step but in making certain that all of the previously introduced steps are being utilized. That is what asking from a position of strength is really all about—the integration of the entirety of ***The System***. One by one, we see the previous steps of ***The System*** coming into play, all of them working together to form a position of strength from which to ask. In this step we more readily recognize the positive results of utilizing all of the steps of ***The System***.

For NFPs to be able to ask from a position of strength they must consistently demonstrate professional standards and ethics. (This topic is addressed more fully in Chapter 12.) It is terribly presumptuous for any NFP that fails to demonstrate attributes of strength to ask for and expect contributions. Embodying professional standards and asking from a position of strength will increase your ability to raise substantial sums of money.

CHAPTER 11

STEP 11: THANK CONTRIBUTORS THREE TIMES BEFORE ASKING AGAIN.

So far this book has concentrated on how to secure a positive response from a donor. This chapter discusses what to do after you receive money or a pledge. How your donors are treated after they have contributed will largely determine how they will respond in the future.

It is a shortsighted fund-raiser who thinks that once the cash or pledge is received the job is done. Not so! Unless the organization asking for funds is in the very unique situation of never needing to ask for additional contributions, fund-raisers must also be concerned about raising money sometime in the immediate or more distant future. If ***The System*** has been adhered to during the solicitation process, donors should be pleased. This chapter deals with what do in between the campaign just completed and the next one.

What should be done? Step 11 of ***The System*** calls for thanking your contributors three times before asking again. Yes, three times! The "thanking process" is crucial.[1] It is not only important to thank contributors, but to thank them in ways that truly demonstrate your appreciation.

This chapter addresses five issues: the benefits of thanking contributors multiple times; different ways to thank contributors; the importance of thanking organizations, foundations, and corporations; pitfalls to avoid when thanking; and the use of thank-you gifts.

Benefits of Thanking Contributors Multiple Times

It is important to thank contributors three times before seeking another contribution. Some may argue that this is overkill or redundant. It is not! Fund-raisers must always be focused on two areas of financial needs: current and long-term. As pointed out in Chapter 6, your known givers are crucial because they are your most likely source for raising more money. It is essential that donors continue to be treated well after a financial campaign so that they will be receptive to the next solicitation for funds.

Using your imagination and creativity in thanking donors three times and in three different ways will definitely reap financial rewards. This procedure ensures that you will stand out in the minds of the contributors as appreciative, concerned, and professional. In fact, you will definitely stand out because few fund-raisers grasp the importance of thanking contributors multiple times.

Different Ways to Thank Contributors

You may thank your donors in a variety of ways: via telephone, letter, e-mail, personal visit, newsletter, to name but a few. But however you do it, it is important that you always thank your donors at least three times and in ways that demonstrate you are personally aware of their individual efforts in this particular fund-raising campaign.

The First Thank you. I find it is most effective to thank donors within the first few days of receiving a contribution. I normally do this in one of three ways: by telephone, letter, or e-mail. I prefer using the telephone or writing a letter, but when I know the preference of the donor is communicating via e-mail, I use that medium.

My first choice is a telephone call. When you have only a few calls to make it is relatively easy to find the time to respond via telephone. If I am involved in a campaign that results in a large number of responses (for example, an annual fund drive) I will devote several days and evenings in a row to making such calls. I can make about twenty calls per hour. I will also involve other appropriate people (board members, officers, paid staff, volunteers) in making the calls.

Reaching a donor's voice mail does not count as a personal contact. In fact, to ensure confidentiality, I do not leave messages on voice mail about contributions that are being contemplated or that have actually been finalized. One never knows for certain who will be accessing the messages and whether the donor wants that person(s) to know about the contribution. Unless a donor has specifically said to leave messages relating to a contribution on voice mail, my advice is never to do it.

If the donor cannot be reached by telephone within the first few days after receiving the contribution, I send a short letter, very briefly thanking the person for his or her support. And, again for confidentiality reasons, a postcard should never be used.

The first thank you (whatever medium is used) needs to be received by the donor as soon after the contribution is received as possible, certainly within ten days.

The Second Thank You. After expressing your initial thank you, Step 11 calls for thanking the donor at least two more times before asking for another contribution. There are a number of ways of doing this, two of which I find to be especially effective.

It is most effective to thank donors in person if you know them by name and see them rather frequently. I do this even when I have been successful in reaching the donor by telephone for the initial thank you. I am not recommending a formal visit or lengthy in-depth conversation—just a brief word during a chance meeting at a social event, a business or service club meeting, before or after church, at the mall or supermarket, etc. I say something like: "Bill, I want you to know how much I and ________ (the name of the charitable entity I am currently representing) appreciate your recent contribution. Your gift will certainly help us. Thanks so much!" If the contribution was made in the name of a husband and wife I add something like: "Please be certain to let Alice know we appreciate her part in this contribution."

I tailor the comments to fit the purpose for which the contribution has been made and the person or persons who were responsible for the contribution. This can also be an effective way of expressing one's appreciation to other family members or to attorneys, accountants, or financial advisors of the donor who assisted in making a contribution a reality. If you are in a public place just be certain that your conversation cannot be overheard. But even in the midst of many people it is usually not difficult to pass on a few confidential comments.

A brief letter is another good option for the "second" thank you. The letter should again thank the donor for the contribution and include a report of what has been accomplished since receiving the contribution. The report may be included in the text of the letter if it is relatively brief. For longer reports, it will be more effective only to refer to the report in the text of the letter and to include a copy of the report with the letter. Keeping your donors apprised of the progress reassures them that their contributions were needed and that you are making good use of their money. They need to know that without their gifts your NFP would not have been able to move forward as it has.

A letter might also announce a milestone completion or show continued progress toward goals. Many donors especially appreciate an enclosed newspaper article or periodical referring to the campaign. If you know in advance there will be radio or TV coverage concerning any of the activities or equipment being funded by their contributions, you can inform your donors of the impending media coverage and thank them again for their contributions. If you do not have advance knowledge of media coverage, you can contact the donors after the fact, saying that their contributions made possible the achievements that attracted the media.

Another alternative is to enclose photographs of activities, of scholarship recipients, of elderly people receiving meals, of a building being built or refurbished, of equipment that has been purchased, of faculty members who have received grants, etc.—all made possible as a result of the donations received.

You may use a number of formal and informal ways to thank your donors the second time. There is no specific timetable for expressing the second thank you; that will be somewhat dependent on the nature and length of the campaign being conducted. It is important, however, that your thank you's are not so scheduled that they become artificial or anticipated by the donor.

The Third Thank You. You can use many of the techniques mentioned above for the "third" thank you. The third thank you can also be a receipt with another brief note thanking the donor.

There are endless possibilities of different ways to thank your contributors. Thinking of ways to thank your contributors three times should be no burden—on the contrary, quite easy.

The Importance of Thanking Organizations, Foundations, and Corporations

Just as you would with an individual donor, it is important to thank donor organizations, foundations, and corporations at least three times before asking again for another donation. And remembering Step 6 (cultivate known givers), you definitely should ask any organization, foundation, or corporation that has contributed to contribute again.

Attention should be given to thanking foundations, corporations, service clubs, organizations, or any group of people who have contributed money, goods, or services. Appearing at a meeting, presenting a plaque, sending letters and reports, and personally thanking officers are appropriate ways of expressing gratitude to organized groups. This should be done whether the contributing organizations are local or out of state. If they contribute, they deserve to be thanked appropriately.

As an added benefit, it is usually relatively easy to get some kind of media coverage (certainly a brief article in a local or regional newspaper or trade magazine) when an organization makes a contribution. This is where your public relations department can be of assistance in helping to thank contributing organizations in ways that really set you apart from all the others.

For some unknown reason, we are more prone to thank individuals for their gifts than we are to thank foundations and corporations. Maybe it is because we think of foundations and corporations in a less personal way—as organizations, not people. One retired executive director of a well-known foundation in California told me that, in most cases, grant recipients were punctual in meeting deadlines for **reporting** on the use of funds received, but they seldom actually **thanked** the foundation. He said when he first began working for the foundation, he felt it was strange not to receive "thank you's," but in later years he became accustomed to it and never expected them.

I asked him if it would make any difference if the foundation were thanked. I still remember his reply: "Why do you think we kept funding your proposals?" The church I served received numerous grants from this foundation, most for correcting many years of deferred maintenance and some for underwriting major programs and salaries of special staff persons, totaling several hundred thousand dollars. I mention these grants because the foundation's guidelines, although not prohibiting them, did not include grants to churches.

I am convinced that we were successful because we followed the steps of ***The System***, including being a standout for thanking the foundation for its continued support. The executive directors of several other foundations told me on various occasions how much their respective organizations appreciated being thanked by me for their grants.

The president of a small steel manufacturing company in a Midwestern city told me that whenever he personally made a charitable contribution, he usually was thanked in some manner, but when the corporation made a contribution, it seldom was thanked except when it had helped one of its own employees. He was the only corporate executive who ever said that to me, but on several occasions corporate board members and officers went out of their way to thank me for my "gracious letter" to them. A vice-president of a fortune 500 company in Minneapolis actually telephoned me one day to thank me for thanking him.

It is just as important to thank foundations and corporations for their charitable gifts as it is to thank individual people or families. Remember that Step 11 calls for thanking three times, even when thanking organizations, foundations, and corporations.

Pitfalls to Avoid When Thanking Donors

There are several pitfalls to avoid when thanking donors. The most common mistakes are failure to personalize letters, omitting the specific gift amount, and soliciting additional money prior to completing three thank you's.

Non-personalized letters are just as much of a "no-no" in the thanking process as they are when asking. The entire thank-you letter should be personalized and signed. With modern technology, it is easy to do. Form letters with a salutation of "Dear *Contributor*" are unacceptable. Writing "Thank you for your *contribution*" is also unsuitable; failing to mention the specific amount of the gift or pledge is objectionable, even when a receipt for the specific amount is included with the letter.

Another common mistake is asking for another contribution, either directly or indirectly, before thanking someone three times. The common practice of enclosing an envelope for mailing one's next contribution with an initial thank you letter violates Step 11. Sometimes an envelope will be enclosed with no mention of it in the text of the letter (which indirectly asks for another contribution), and sometimes the letter will specifically refer to using the "enclosed envelope for your next contribution" (directly requesting a future contribution). Regardless of the intent, including an envelope can create the appearance of being presumptuous—of taking donors for granted. Based on interviews with donors as well as off-hand comments I have overheard, I believe that many donors perceive that they have been taken for granted and resent being treated as "cash cows." Clearly not all donors feel this way, but fund-raisers should proceed with caution. If any procedure used in the total fund-raising and thanking process offends even a small percentage of your giving base, it is best to re-evaluate and find a more effective method.

Thank-You Gifts in Return for Contributions

Receiving gifts in return for one's donations is a touchy subject because donors' reactions to this procedure differ widely. The major criticism leveled against the procedure is made by those who contend that the NFP should keep the complete donation and not spend money on gifts. They assert that donors have contributed in support of the mission of the NFP and not to buy or receive gifts. Those who make this case usually feel strongly about it.

Gift giving, however, is an integral part of some fund-raising plans. That is the case with Dr. Robert Schuller, mentioned in Chapter 7 as being a masterful fund-raiser. He has been unusually successful in raising money for nearly half a century, and he consistently sends gifts—many of them very lovely and unique that could not be easily purchased elsewhere—in return for contributions. When he solicits contributions, he goes into considerable detail describing the gifts. He is also very careful to announce that the gifts have been specially designed and manufactured *free of charge* to the Crystal Cathedral to be used in this way.

Criticism associated with sending gifts is minimized if the NFP does not have any direct out-of-pocket expenses associated with obtaining and mailing the gifts. NFPs must be sensitive about offending their giving base, and they need to determine if more money is raised or lost by giving gifts.

I find no fault with sending gifts in return for contributions as long as the costs associated with the "thanking-gifts' programs" are underwritten by an outside entity and as long as the gifts are in good taste—not cheap or tacky. It is important that the gifts fairly represent the character of the NFPs sending them. (Cheap ballpoint pens that do not work are a real turnoff, especially if not enough postage has been used and the donor has to pay "postage due.")

Closely associated with giving gifts is the practice of public memorials, using plaques or bricks with the names of donors inscribed on them to acknowledge or commemorate the givers. The plaques, of various sizes and materials, are placed in conspicuous places on or nearby walls, doors, corner stones, or windows; inscriptions are placed on musical instruments, pieces of equipment or furniture, picture frames, works of art, outside benches, sidewalks, statues, etc. In response to large gifts, a room, a section of a building, or an entire building may be named after the donor. In most instances prospective donors know what levels of giving are required in order to be thanked or recognized in these ways. In previous years, it was not uncommon for an entire college to be named after a donor in gratitude for a very substantial financial gift. Although current construction costs make that a practice of by-gone days, some of today's colleges and universities still bear the names of their original benefactors.

A less permanent way of publicly recognizing and thanking contributors is listing their names in monthly, quarterly, or annual publications.

Frequently their names will be included with a specific category of givers based on the dollar amount of the gifts. The sponsors of special events can be publicly thanked by including a notice of their sponsorship on the programs of such occasions or by appropriate signage at the events. This is especially common for concerts, plays, art exhibitions, auctions, charity horse shows, flower expositions, photography contests, sporting events, etc. These less permanent ways of thanking donors appear to be very popular with the majority of both donors and donees.

Some critics contend that publicly thanking donors amounts to "buying recognition" and should not be considered a legitimate fund-raising practice. Others contend that the practice is necessary in order to attract the funds necessary to carry on their work. And many believe that the great majority of people give to NFPs because they believe in the cause, not for recognition. My opinion is irrelevant. The only thing that really matters is how your NFP and donors feel about it. Every fund-raiser needs to give this matter careful consideration when developing the fund-raising plan (Step 1).

Conclusion

Although thanking is the last step of the fund-raising process, it is an essential part of every fund-raising project. The thanking process should not be an afterthought or a tag-on responsibility that is given little attention. Instead, it should be thought of as the first step of the next fund-raising campaign.

How your donors are treated after they have contributed will determine, to no small degree, how they will respond in the future. The thanking process should be executed with as much energy and care as the asking process. Step 11 is crucial to your long-term fund-raising success. And remember what I said in the introduction about deviating from the entirety of ***The System***. The more you deviate, the less likely you are to succeed in reaching your funding goals. Or positively stated, the more you adhere to ***The System*** the more likely you are to succeed.

Remember that Step 11 calls for thanking your donors **three times** before asking them for another contribution.

NOTE TO CHAPTER 11

1. Thomas Wolf makes a very strong argument for the necessity of thanking donors time and again. See Wolf's book, *Managing A Nonprofit Organization*, published by Prentice Hall Press, 1990, p. 227.

CHAPTER 12

STEP 12: ALWAYS ADHERE TO PROFESSIONAL STANDARDS OF FUND-RAISING.

We are a society that tends to make snap judgments. Right or wrong, we form first impressions when we meet people. Sometimes our first impressions are correct, and other times they are incorrect. We fund-raisers need to keep in mind that prospective donors frequently make quick judgments about NFPs and the way they ask for money.

Step 12 of ***The System*** is **always adhere to professional standards of fund-raising**. The emphasis is upon "professional." Two stories emphasize the importance.

While attending graduate school at the University of St. Andrews in Scotland, I was married with two children. Our one-year old son became ill, and we needed a doctor. Under Great Britain's socialized medicine program, medical care was paid for by the British government for American students studying in that country. Although free, we did not have the luxury of selecting our doctor. The usual procedure was to telephone the healthcare district office, and the nurse would decide whether you would go to the doctor's office or if a doctor would come to you.

The nurse decided to send a doctor to our house. A very young doctor who had just graduated from medical school was assigned to us. He appeared at our doorstep without a doctor's bag. His arms were full of the paraphernalia a doctor needs to make an initial examination (stethoscope, blood pressure apparatus, reflex hammer, box of tongue depressors, light reflector with leather strap for his head, etc.), and his pockets were bulging with bottles of pills and liquid medicines and other equipment. He was quite a sight!

He may have been a very qualified doctor, but his lack of professional demeanor and appearance detracted from his ability to inspire confidence in his patients and hindered his effectiveness as a doctor. Even before he had the opportunity to examine our son, we questioned his medical expertise.

Years later, when I was the president of a small college, I had an early afternoon appointment with two men who wanted the college to purchase some curriculum materials that their company had recently developed. On that day, it poured down rain. The college's parking lot was about 50 yards from the entrance to the administration building where my office was located. The two men did not have umbrellas and decided to make a run for the administration building.

They misjudged both the intensity of the rain and the time it would take to navigate the flight of steps leading to the front door. The stone steps, which had worn unevenly over the 100 plus years they had been in use, were sixteen inches deep and only four inches high, making it necessary to take many more steps than anticipated. The men were soaked when they got to my secretary's office. When I came out of my office to meet them each was standing in a puddle and water was dripping off their rain-soaked hair and running down their faces. I suggested that we postpone the meeting for a couple of hours so they could go back to their motel and change. But they had been on the road for three days making presentations to other colleges and had left their clothes at a hotel in a city about three hours away where they were scheduled to meet their wives that night.

We had little choice other than to meet. However, the distractions proved too much, and the meeting was not very productive. These two men had traveled 350 miles from another state to make an important presentation to a college president whom they had never met, and all any of us could focus on was how wet they were. To this day, I do not know whether or not they had a quality product; I could not get past their lack of professionalism. One may say that it was not their fault. Of course it was—any professional knows the importance of listening to weather reports and having an umbrella in one's car for an unexpected rainy day.

These two stories demonstrate that both your appearance and your knowledge of the products or services being offered help constitute your professional demeanor and your ability to instill confidence and goodwill in others. There are many professional customs and ethics that we learn on our own and others that people teach us.

Learning about professionalism

I remember my father giving me a briefcase in my senior year of college. This was in the days before backpacks, and students just carried their books. On a college campus only law students and "nerds" used a briefcase. I could not bring myself to tell my father that I could not use it, so I just quietly stored it away. (I was being as absurd as the young doctor in Scotland.) One day in graduate school, I started using it on a daily basis "because I had too many books to carry." Besides, in graduate school, all the students carried a briefcase.

I had a similar experience with carrying an umbrella. As an undergraduate I thought that only girls used umbrellas. (I was being as silly as the two men making a run for my office from the parking lot.) But one day in graduate school I announced that "it rained more in Connecticut than it did in Missouri," and I bought myself an umbrella.

What caused me to change my practiced norms where a briefcase and umbrella were concerned? Perhaps I just grew up. As Paul writes in I Corinthians 13:11, "When I was a child . . . I reasoned like a child; when I became a man, I gave up childish ways." Or maybe it was being exposed to the more professional atmosphere of a graduate school that was focused on a particular profession. Maybe it was just using good common sense. Who knows why it happened? What matters is that it did happen.

What I am suggesting is that some of one's understanding of professional standards comes from being exposed to them and adopting them as your own. But ethics and accepted norms of practices are too important just to be left to chance. If you are serious about being a fund-raiser, you must be proactive in learning as much as possible about professionalism as it relates specifically to fund-raising.

The purpose of this chapter is to discuss the importance of ethics and standards in fund-raising, to suggest some sources for learning more about professionalism, and to call attention to nine principals of a true fund-raising professional.

Fund-Raising Standards and Ethics

Most professions have their own standards, ethics, and accepted norms of practices. Frequently people in one profession may not be aware of or fully understand the ethical standards of another. Many professions have written and/or unwritten ethics and standards that have been formulated and modified over time. Some professions have one main governing body (like the American Bar Association for attorneys and the American Medical Association for medical doctors), while others have more than one organization competing for membership.

There are several organizations, agencies, and companies that are directly or indirectly connected with fund-raising. A majority of them have published their own codes of behavior or ethics or have endorsed someone else's. The National Society of Fund Raising Executives (NSFRE) is probably the best known and celebrated of the professional organizations for individual membership. The first paragraph of its *Code of Ethical Principles and Standards of Professional Practice: Statement of Ethical Principles* states that it "exists to foster the development and growth of fund-raising professionals and the profession, to preserve and enhance philanthropy and volunteerism, and to promote high ethical standards in the fund-raising profession."

Many other highly respected organizations and agencies engaged in some phase of fund-raising subscribe to specific codes of professional behavior and ethics. The following is a list of the better known of these groups, most of which have their own websites:

- American Association of Fundraising Counsel (AAFRC), respected especially for its diligent work each year in researching and publishing *Giving USA*,
- American Council on Gift Annuities (ACGA),
- Association for Healthcare Philanthropy (AHP),

- Council for Advancement and Support of Education (CASE),
- Association of Fundraising Professionals (AFP),
- The Canaras Group,
- Independent Sector,
- National Catholic Development Conference (NCDC),
- National Committee on Planned Giving (NCPG),
- National Council for Resource Development (NCRD), and
- United Way of America.

A copy of *A Donor Bill Of Rights*—developed jointly by AAFRC, AHP, CASE, and AFP and endorsed by nearly all of the other organizations and agencies—can be found on page 235 of *Giving USA 2003*. Copies of four significant codes can be found in "Appendix F" (pages 393-397) of *Practical Guide to Planned Giving 2000* (eighth edition), edited by Paul H. Schneiter and published by The Taft Group. They are: *Model Standards of Practice for the Charitable Gift Planner* (adopted by NCPG and ACGA in 1991), *The Canaras Code* (drafted in 1990 by the Canaras Group), *Code of Ethical Principles and Standards of Professional Practice: Statements of Ethical Principles* (adopted by NSFRE in 1991), and *Standards of Professional Practice* (adopted by NSFRE in 1992 and incorporated into its 1991 *Code*).

You can begin to develop an appreciation for and understanding of the most important aspects of professionalism in fund-raising by carefully studying all five of the documents mentioned above, along with any other codes that you may find. In addition to being familiar with the codes of various organizations, I highly recommend that you go to the next level and formulate your own personal code of ethics and mission statement. It is helpful to formulate hard and fast rules of professional practices that you are totally committed to and will comply with regardless of the situation or circumstances.

Nine Fund-Raising Principles of Professionalism

There are nine essential behavioral principles that distinguish a true fund-raising professional. These are in addition to the cornerstones of integrity and honesty that fund-raisers are expected to build on and practice under all circumstances. The nine fundamentals that guide the behavior of a professional fund-raiser are:

1. Look and act like a professional,
2. Avoid percentage or commission-based compensation,
3. Use contributions properly,
4. Actively seek assistance from other professionals,
5. Keep confidences,
6. Establish realistic priorities and expectations,
7. Share the glory and accept the blame,
8. Continue education and professional development, and
9. Maintain a work-life balance.

1. Look and act like a professional. This obviously goes beyond briefcases and umbrellas. It deals with your professional presence, image, and reputation. It includes the tangibles and intangibles, the obvious and the subtle. I have seen major gifts lost as the result of the fund-raiser's unprofessional appearance, lack of social graces, and failure to adhere to commonly recognized moral standards of behavior.

Physically, it is the way we dress, groom, and present ourselves. It is important to dress appropriately for the group with whom we are working or from whom we are seeking contributions. A professional dresses in good taste for social events, which, depending upon the occasion, can range from formal attire to business, to business casual, to casual. Keeping shoes polished and clothes cleaned and pressed are also important. Having one's hair properly groomed, nails cut, and appropriate makeup are significant aspects of looking like professionals. And using lotions and perfumes with appropriate scents should not be overlooked. We should never need to apologize for the way we look, and no colleague should ever feel the need to apologize for us.

Social graces are also important, such things as knowing how to shake hands, how to meet and introduce people, the appropriate way to address a person with a title or army rank, how to RSVP to an invitation, and good table manners. I know of more than one major gift that was lost as the result of a fund-raiser being asked to dine at a prospective donor's home and having no grasp of good dining etiquette. If you are shaky in any of these areas, I strongly recommend that you purchase a recently written book on basic social and business etiquette. There are several good ones available through any major bookstore.

Social graces and professionalism also extend to the use of appropriate language. Profanity and off-color jokes in speeches and personal conversations offend many people, yet some fundraisers cannot seem to refrain from using them. The use of any language that implies bias of race, gender, ethnic origin, religion or politics (when used in a non-religious or non-political arena), etc. must be avoided. Most seasoned professionals will confess that they have used profanity or off-color jokes only to find that they were counterproductive. There is no need to risk a prospective donor's feeling embarrassed or becoming angry with or disappointed in you or the NFP you represent.

Many people also judge professionals by their moral conduct. Becoming romantically involved with a donor or donor's spouse is a definite "no-no" that will frequently lead to a multitude of devastating results, including loss of contribution, loss of job, and loss of reputation. Office romances are likewise a mistake that can have professional repercussions for more people than those involved. I know of a college president who was asked to retire early because he tried to cover-up the romantic involvement of his secretary with the director of development, both of whom were married. I have known of the credibility of an entire development program being called into question over extramarital affairs of one development executive. Careers are lost, NFPs called into question, and reputations ruined over these issues. I will not even attempt to address the pain it causes many families.

There are some free-spirited people who think the emphasis upon dress, social graces, and morality is old-fashioned and of little relevance to today's fund-raiser. Displaying good manners and proper language are always appropriate forms of behavior for professional fund-raisers. It is also important to remember that the great majority of major deferred gifts come from older people, most of whom have a high regard for what may be viewed as old-fashioned values.

2. Avoid percentage or commission-based compensation. Organizations not acquainted with professional fund-raising norms and practices frequently request that fund-raisers be compensated on a percentage or commission basis. New organizations or those that are raising money for the first time tend to favor compensating fund-raisers on a commission basis. It appears to be a safe route to follow. If money is raised they will pay a percentage to the fund-raiser; if no money is raised, no fees are paid. But fund-raisers being paid a finder's fee or a percentage of philanthropic funds donated is an absolute "no-no." This is considered to be an unethical practice among all development professionals and all professional organizations related to fund-raising.

Every code of professional ethics and procedures I know of clearly condemns such a practice. Fund-raisers on all levels should be paid a salary or set fee that is reasonable and proportionate to the services provided, and the compensation should be paid by the NFP for which the services are provided.

Commission-based pay for fund-raisers has historically led to many misunderstandings, uncertainties, and changes in focus. For starters, it seems a little unfair to expect the donor to pay a commission in addition to his or her willingness to make a charitable contribution, and most donors do not want their donations going toward commissions. Donors realize that it costs money to raise money, but they expect those expenses to be part of the general administrative budget of the recipient NFP. It is important to keep donors happy and for NFPs to consider the long-term consequences of paying commissions on contributions.

There are short-term disadvantages, as well. At first glance it may seem like a good deal for the NFP; if no money is raised, no commissions are paid. But when fund-raisers skirt around the accepted norms and get paid by commissions, they usually receive from 20% to 35% of the contributions they raise. The NFP pays all other administrative expenses, such as printing, postage, telephone, entertainment, and travel. This means that if your goal is to net $25,000, you will need to raise between $30,000 and $33,000, plus expenses, as well as meet your regular payroll and office expenses. That is no bargain for the NFP and well in excess of the normal administrative expenses incurred by most NFPs for their fund-raising.

Commission-based compensation is especially difficult for deferred gifts because many of the funds will not be received for years. Very few fund-raisers will be willing to wait several years to receive their commissions. That places the NFP in the position of paying commissions for money yet to be received, which might well create a cash-flow shortage. With most trusts, the NFP will not know how much money it will receive until the trust expires and the organization receives the "remainder" of the funds. Do you estimate or guess at how much commission is to be paid?

It is also difficult for immediate gifts, especially those surrounding annual-fund campaigns, where prospective contributors **pledge** to pay their annual gift over a 12-month period. Again, fund-raisers are not willing to have their commissions dribble in over a period of months, and many pledges are not ultimately honored, which means an NFP can lose money if it pays commissions in advance. If a fund-raiser is being paid on commission, he or she is most likely to concentrate on immediate gifts that will assure an immediate and exact commission, creating a limited focus and imbalance in the total development effort.

Almost all foundations are opposed to commission-based pay. Most application forms for foundation grants have a disclosure box to be checked if the person preparing the foundation proposal is to receive compensation based on a percentage of the grant awarded. If the box is checked, most foundations will automatically reject the proposal.

If an organization has a limited development staff and periodically needs additional assistance, consultants or temporary personnel should be secured and paid an exact pre-determined fee for their services. I can think of no circumstance that warrants paying a commission for a charitable contribution.

3. Use contributions properly. Another important consideration is the proper use of contributions. Without exception, contributions should be used for the purposes that the recipient NFPs designated at the time the donations were solicited or for the purposes the donors designated when they contributed the gifts and the NFPs accepted them. NFPs (even well-known, distinguished ones) destroy their credibility with current and prospective donors by failing to use the monies contributed in exactly the ways the donors had been told or led to believe. If the NFP decides, for whatever reason, that it wants or needs to use the money for different purposes than originally anticipated, it should seek the permission of the contributors. If a good case is made for changing the focus, donors usually agree. If a donor does not agree, the NFP should, without any feelings of ill will, either use the money for the original purpose or offer to return the contribution to the donor.

People have the right to spend their money as they choose. If you let prospective donors decide how much to contribute, the best way to contribute the money, and how the gift is to be used, you will frequently be surprised at how "on point" their decisions will be. And this does not mean they do not need your input.

It is important to "tell it like it is" when dealing with donors. There is no acceptable excuse for not being absolutely honest with donors at all times. I have seen numerous attempts at shading the truth, misleading donors or, at best, trying to guide them to do what the recipient NFP wants with little concern for the best interests of the donors. Integrity is of the utmost importance when dealing with people's money. It is especially easy to exaggerate the tax benefits of a gift or encourage a gift of a particular nature because it benefits the institution or organization. However, the true professional will always focus on the welfare and overall good of the donor.

It has been my experience that as long as everyone involved deals in complete honesty with one another, any discord that may arise between a donee and donor can usually be resolved to the mutual satisfaction of both parties. After all, both parties are trying to accomplish the same thing; the prospective contributor wants to contribute a gift to be used in responsible ways, and the NFP wants to receive funds to use for creditable purposes.

In the end, it is most important for the donor to feel good about his or her contribution and its intended purpose.

4. Actively seek assistance from other professionals. The true professional will always welcome and solicit the assistance of other professionals when dealing with difficult situations. Your best ideas may well come from another person, or another person could catch a mistake you are about to make. Unfortunately, there are many who consider it a weakness to seek help from others, and an equal number who think they know everything and try to dominate the entire scene. But a team effort will usually produce the best results.

It is especially important to have on your team people representing donors. Believe me, I know that it can be tedious working with contributors' lawyers, accountants, financial advisors, guardians, etc., but they are charged with the professional responsibility of looking after the best interests of their clients, your potential contributors. If you really care about the well being of your donors, you will encourage the involvement of others who know them and their circumstances much better than you do.

A true fund-raising professional will actively seek the input of other professionals.

5. Keep confidences. One of the highest compliments a fund-raiser can be paid is being thought of as a confidant. Confidentiality and integrity are watchwords among development professionals. There is absolutely no place in fund-raising circles for gossip or sharing privileged information. Whenever a fund-raiser wants to share secrets with me about the private affairs of an institution, donor, or other fund-raiser, I steer clear of that person because I know that he or she cannot be trusted and will likely share privileged information about me with others.

6. Establish realistic priorities and expectations. Not having enough time and hurrying seems to be an epidemic that runs throughout all levels of life in the United States. In the first chapter I talked about executives who are just too busy to sit and think or go on retreats and about college students always waiting until the last minute to write their term papers. Each of us has experienced this. It takes longer to do things than we anticipate, and we have more things to do than we have time for. Because of this, it is crucial for development professionals to budget their time and set priorities so that they can complete the many details that are crucial for successful fund-raising.

I have witnessed and participated in too many hectic scenes as grant-seekers try to meet a foundation-proposal deadline. Most are very similar. People wait until the last minute to complete a chart, to substantiate statistics, to secure the needed binders, to get a signature, etc. The copy machine runs out of toner or there is not enough of the special paper needed to make the proposal really look nice. It is off to Kinko's for a hurry-up job. There are those last minute, frantic trips to the post office or FedEx; this is the last day for a postmark or the proposal has to be received by tomorrow. And then all too frequently there is the discovery (too late to do anything about) that a graph has been omitted, an estimate miscalculated, a signature is needed in more than one place or by more than one officer, the instructions say not to bind the proposal, or more than one copy is called for, and on the list goes. Too often, proposals get botched because people do not plan ahead or allow enough time to meet deadlines. Professionals will budget their time and set priorities, making certain that they have the time needed to complete in a timely manner the many details that are so crucial for successful fund-raising.

When seeking a contribution submitting or distributing inaccurate information is the "kiss of death." Individuals, foundations, and corporations rightly expect charitable organizations of all kinds and sizes to keep faultless records and to provide accurate information. It is risky to respond hurriedly over the telephone to inquiries involving facts and figures. You may make an error or the callers may misunderstand you. This is especially the case for people who telephone for specific information about deferred-giving vehicles. It is best to take the time required to supply inquirers with written information that you have personally checked and re-checked for accuracy.

Setting unrealistic expectations can also be a problem. Through the years, I have probably been guilty of expecting too much of myself and of setting goals that border on being unrealistically high. I remember when I first began working as the development officer of a community college that the president asked me to project how much money I thought the college would raise during the first 12 months of the new development program. When I gave him the figure, he thought I was $200,000 too high. I encouraged him to trust my judgment and to include the figure in his proposed budget, but he decided to split the difference in the figure he submitted to the board. I was determined to reach my initial figure. Although I met the goal, I worked day and night and weekends, and in hindsight, the quality of my work suffered. I should have been more realistic in setting my short- and long-term expectations. Had I been more realistic, I would have accomplished the same things, but just a little later.

If you are to be consistently effective over the course of your career as a fund-raiser, it is imperative that you are disciplined enough to establish and adhere to realistic priorities and expectations. This will enable you to pay meticulous attention to every aspect of your fund-raising projects and will help distinguish you as a genuine professional.

7. Share the glory and accept the blame. When I was in high school, football quarterbacks called their own plays. We had a quarterback who, when our team was in scoring position, consistently called a play that gave him the opportunity to carry the ball across the goal line. As I remember, he had twice as many touchdowns as his closest rival. Although I was not on the football team, it bothered me that he consistently put himself in the limelight. I liken him to the professor on the college campus who uses graduate students to assist in the research that is necessary for writing an article or book but never gives the students any credit. As long as I can remember, I have disliked attracting attention to one's self at the expense of others who are also deserving of credit.

A true professional knows that teamwork is a necessary ingredient for successful fund-raising. Giving recognition to all who have participated, regardless of what part they played, breeds good will and high morale and paves the way for success with future campaigns. The professional fund-raiser will share the limelight with others who have helped in raising money. And the team can be rather broad-based: professionals from other fields, volunteers, retired staff members with special expertise, alumni, students, other administrative staff, board members, and paid consultants.

The flip side is that professionals must also accept the blame when contributions are less than expected and goals are not met. Development personnel have a way of thinking that they can absolve themselves of any blame by pointing their fingers at others. The most common scapegoats are "unqualified volunteers," "lazy staff personnel," "members of the governing board," or the "president." A true fund-raising professional, however, will share both the glory and the blame. When you are willing to do this, you will be more effective and insightful and others will hold you in higher esteem.

8. Continue education and professional development. It is essential for all levels of fund-raisers to keep up-to-date. It is very dangerous when fund-raisers do not know the latest information in fund-raising. Not only do they lose out on opportunities to raise substantially more money, they also risk making mistakes with donor contributions. Most of us have heard horror stories about donors being given incorrect information that led to unfortunate tax consequences. Fund-raisers must be up-to-date on the latest rules and regulations.

As we grow older and are more experienced, we tend to think that we do no not need to attend training seminars and professional conferences. Rules and regulations can change ever so slightly, and if we are unaware of those changes we may unintentionally give faulty advice or make incorrect decisions regarding taxes, various giving vehicles, etc. I recommend that **every** fund-raiser attend no fewer than two training seminars or professional conferences per year—three if possible.

I also recommend that you sign up as soon as you receive the workshop, seminar, or conference information. Most of us know all too well that if we wait to register until we are certain that we have the time to attend, we usually will determine that we are too busy. We also know how tempting it is to think seriously about canceling at the last minute. But I can honestly say that I benefit from every professional seminar, training session, or conference I attend. I always learn something that proves to be useful in my work, meet someone who gives me a new perspective on what I am doing, or become aware of new resources available to my colleagues and me. Attending such meetings is a very significant aspect of being a professional.

Finally, it is crucial that we take the time necessary to keep up-to-date on our professional reading. Remember the story of the minister at the beginning of Chapter 1—it takes a disciplined person to set aside time on a regular basis for reading that helps keep us up-to-date professionally. It is also a very significant ingredient for success.

9. Maintain a work-life balance. Fund-raising is a time-consuming job, and most fund-raisers regularly work more than a 40-hour week. Being a development professional is tedious, exacting, and often stressful. But true professionals avoid becoming burnout victims. You need to take time to relax, unwind, and rejuvenate. Most of us know that it can be hard to take more than two or three vacation days every now and then. But it is important to take off long enough to enjoy an honest-to-goodness vacation—preferably at least two uninterrupted weeks. I have spent time with overworked fund-raisers who have not taken a real vacation for years, and it is not a pleasant experience.

If you fall into this category (as I have from time to time), either you need to change your work habits or your job description needs to be altered to allow for well-deserved vacation time. Burning the candle at both ends over an extended period definitely will prove to be counterproductive. Your productivity will suffer, your disposition will become noticeably less tranquil, and others will begin to notice those unattractive bags under your eyes. And the real tragedy is that you will be trying so hard to do a good job that you may be the last person to recognize that your career is suffering or possibly unraveling. If you are a professional fund-raiser, you will not allow yourself to become a burnout victim or a person whom your family and friends seldom see.

Conclusion

Step 12 of ***The System*** calls for all individuals participating in development activity to adhere to professional standards of fund-raising at all times. This is not always easy. Most people will encounter tempting circumstances that will test their credibility. Unprofessional and indiscreet actions by fund-raisers will come back to haunt them; such actions somehow have a way of becoming public. And once fund-raisers get the reputation of being indiscreet, insincere, or unprofessional, their effectiveness is severally hampered and can probably never be completely restored. The best way to avoid these difficult situations is always being certain that you are, in every way, a professional.

Step 12 differs from the other steps. Although the other steps work together to form a unified system, each step depicts a separate action (for example, Plan your work, Believe in the cause, Think of yourself as a matchmaker, etc). Step 12, on the other hand, is an ingredient of each of the other steps. Step 12 calls for being professional as you Plan your work, Believe in the cause, Think of your self as a matchmaker, etc. This step does not stand-alone and has no real relevance if it is not connected with one or more of the other "action" steps. This step influences the other steps and serves as their foundation; each step demands professionalism to be successful.

This step could have been either the first or last chapter of the book. I chose to place it here because I thought it would be better understood if seen in the context of the entirety of ***The System***. Without this step, the other steps lack heart and conviction. Step 12 gives the entire system its backbone and character. All of the other steps, as powerful and useful as they are, would be sadly lacking if they were not laced with professionalism. Professionalism is the glue that holds all the steps together and enables ***The System*** to stand the test of time.

CONCLUSION

As you have probably guessed by now, I am passionate about fund-raising and the role that non-profits play in our country. The more money we raise, the more lives we can affect. I must confess, I get a rush each time a check arrives in the mail or a pledge is made.

Whether you are in the early stages of your career and looking for a lot of guidance or you are an experienced fund-raiser hoping to pick up a few tips, I hope this book has given you new ideas, provided inspiration, and outlined a strategy that will make you more effective.

A friend of mine recently said to me, "You are a really good story teller." I have told you the many stories in this book for three primary reasons:

1. They help emphasize that ***The System*** has evolved over a period of time from real-life experiences in the fund-raising world;
2. They demonstrate that when fund-raisers deviate from ***The System*** the results of their fund-raising efforts will be diminished; and
3. They affirm that ***The System*** works.

The System has helped me raise millions of dollars during my career, and I know it will also work for you if you follow the steps. ***The System*** definitely works, but checks do not automatically arrive in your mailbox, foundations do not rush to fund your various needs, and prospective donors do not clamor to meet with you. These things do happen, but they are the result of meticulously working through **all** of the steps of ***The System***.

Although we have examined each step individually, it is helpful to view all twelve of the steps together in a single list:

Step 1: Plan your work, and work your plan.
Step 2: Believe in the cause.

Step 3: Think of yourself as a matchmaker.
Step 4: Concentrate on the number of gifts instead of the dollar amounts of gifts.
Step 5: Develop and test your mailing lists.
Step 6: Cultivate known givers.
Step 7: Ask to receive.
Step 8: Encourage using assorted giving vehicles and gifts.
Step 9: Emphasize project support.
Step 10: Always ask from a position of strength.
Step 11: Thank contributors three times before asking again.
Step 12: Always adhere to professional standards of fund-raising.

It is absolutely essential that you follow each and every step of ***The System***. This is not a matter of selecting one or more and ignoring the others. The title of each step is self-explanatory and cuts to the core of that step. There really is not much else to be said about any of the steps with the exception of Step 1: *Plan your work, and work your plan*.

It is not by accident that this step is placed first. Planning is where all fund-raising begins. Through the years I have observed that the most prevalent cause for failing to reach one's fund-raising potential is not preparing written fund-raising plans. I do not want to be guilty of belaboring any one step, but Step 1 is so crucial that it is appropriate to take one last look at it.

Although each and every step is important, you must begin with solid planning. Regardless of the size of your NFP or its mission, you need one umbrella plan that relates to all phases of fund-raising for the organization or institution, and another plan for each individual fund-raising event.[1] If you are part of a larger and more complex NFP with several different campaigns being executed, you will need an individual plan that flows back to your umbrella plan for each fund-raising event.

Both very small and very large organizations frequently make the same mistake. Smaller NFPs with few staff members, a meager budget, and limited outreach mistakenly think that their fund-raising activities are so modest that a written plan is not necessary. Very large organizations with multiple staff members having decades of combined experience mistakenly assume they are so well-informed and experienced that no written plans are needed. In both cases the assumptions are totally false. Regardless of the magnitude of the fund-raising endeavor, **written fund-raising plans are essential for successful results**.

Many people do not formulate fund-raising plans because they are intimidated by the thought of having to put them down on paper. Do not let this thought put you off. A fund-raising plan is not for public consumption. It is meant as a guide for **you to use** in executing your fund-raising undertaking. Do not get bogged down in worrying about what others are going to think of your plan—about how your plan looks or how well it reads. I have seen many very effective fund-raising plans that consist of nothing more than one-liners in outline form. I have seen very well conceived plans that have been written on the back of a conference program during dull sessions. It is not uncommon to see plans that were initially scribbled on napkins in a coffee shop late at night as several fund-raisers got together after a long day at a seminar or training session. A fund raising plan does not have to be fancy—it just has to be.

Most fund-raisers agree that the hardest part of any fund-raising plan is getting it started. My best suggestion is not to pay attention to the form or order of your recorded thoughts. Just brainstorm, either by yourself or with others. Let your mind go wherever it wants and record your thoughts in any fashion that makes it possible for you to recall what you have been thinking. Once you get your initial thoughts recorded you can organize, edit, and rework them into a logical and practical fund-raising plan that can be used as a blueprint by you or others. After the initial two or three paragraphs of a fund-raising plan are written, you will be surprised at how easily the rest of it falls into place.

Trying to raise money without a plan is like trying to drive a car without starting the motor. The plan is what drives all fund-raising efforts. Its importance cannot be overemphasized. It is the foundation upon which your fund-raising efforts are built. But one step alone, regardless of its importance, is not sufficient. Properly executing all the steps of ***The***

System is crucial for the successful realization of one's fund-raising goals.

In the *Introduction,* I compared the steps of ***The System*** to the "entire network of checklists" that pilots of commercial airlines use. The checklists are used to make certain that the captain and first officer do everything that is required for taking off and landing safely, and the steps of ***The System*** are used to make absolutely certain that every step needed for successful fund-raising is taken, than none is accidentally omitted.[2]

Dr. Harry Wong is well known to teachers across America for his practical and motivational presentations at major conferences. Many young teachers are given copies of his book *The First Days of School,* as a guide to assist them in their first teaching experiences. Interestingly enough, veteran teachers have reported that the book has been an equally valuable tool for them. It serves as a reminder of basic practices they may have unintentionally abandoned along the way as new classroom routines were developed and shortcuts taken.[3] Similarly, ***The System*** can be an equally valuable tool for fund-raisers of all levels of experience.

The checklists that pilots use are "challenge-and-response" checklists—that is, one person reads the item to be checked and the other responds. This procedure was designed to make certain that flight crews adhere to every one of the items on the checklists every time they fly.

I have devised my own "challenge-and-response" process for adhering, without exception, to all steps of ***The System***. I use it every time I participate in a fund-raising campaign. I use worksheets that list each of the steps of ***The System***. Under each step I place one line for me to check, initial, and date. Under that line I leave room to write one relatively short paragraph.

- The first line—which calls for a checkmark, date, and initial—is my acknowledgment that I have completed that step. Including a place for the date and my initials is a way of certifying—as a professional fund-raiser—that I have completed that step in its totality. By placing my initial there I am putting my reputation on the line.

- The space for a paragraph is for me to provide a short summary of what I did in adhering to that particular step. I emphasize both the words "short" and "summary." These worksheets are not the plan or blueprint—they are my "challenge-and-response" process for making certain that ***The System*** is being followed.

This is the process **I** use. It is important that **you** develop your own process for verifying that all twelve steps of ***The System*** are being adhered to. Adhering to ***The System*** in its entirety will enable you to become a very successful and professional raiser of funds for charitable purposes.

I was a middle-distance runner in high school and college. To be competitive it took year-round training that consisted of intensive hours of hard work to prepare for relatively brief periods of actually running in races—just a little under two minutes for the half mile and a little over four minutes for the mile run. That never bothered me because of the pure joy and sense of achievement experienced when breaking the tape at the end of a race.

Being a professional fund-raiser is much like being an athlete—it takes arduous hours of intense preparation and follow-up in comparison to the short time that is actually spent in asking for and receiving contributions. But that never bothers me for two reasons. First, I experience a similar joy and sense of achievement in being a member of a successful fund-raising team as I did as a member of a winning track team. However, there is one main difference. There were so few track meets to remember; there is a lifetime of fund-raising experiences to remember. Second, it is exhilarating—far beyond that experienced in winning a race—to do something that really makes a difference in the lives of people, individually and collectively. And raising money for charitable organizations and institutions does just that.

It is incredibly satisfying to be a professional fund-raiser and to be a member of the team that helps relieve suffering and assists in bringing greater happiness, meaning, and fulfillment into the lives of individuals and large segments of people. I believe that is what being a real winner in life is all about. And if that is what you want your life to be all about, ***The System*** is for you!

NOTES TO THE CONCLUSION

1. Chapter 1, p. 14.
2. Introduction, p. 6.
3. Observation provided by Dr. Velma Saire, well-known educator who lives in Pittsburgh, PA.

INDEX